PEGGY GUGGENHEIM

Peggy Guggenheim

The Shock of the Modern

FRANCINE PROSE

Yale

UNIVERSITY

PRESS

New Haven and London

Yale University Press books may be purchased in quantity for educational,
business, or promotional use. For information, please e-mail sales.press@yale.edu
(U.S. office) or sales@yaleup.co.uk (U.K. office).

Set in Janson Oldstyle type by Integrated Publishing Solutions.
Printed in the United States of America.

Library of Congress Control Number: 2015932202
ISBN 978-0-300-20348-6 (cloth : alk. paper)

A catalogue record for this book is available from the British Library.

This paper meets the requirements of ANSI/NISO Z39.48-1992
(Permanence of Paper).

10 9 8 7 6 5 4 3 2

In writing about Peggy it's important to listen to one's own instinct. Don't listen to critics. What do they know? What one should say about Peggy is, simply, that she did it. That no matter what her motivations were, she did it.
—Lee Krasner

———————

I am not an art collector. I am a museum.
—Peggy Guggenheim

CONTENTS

CONTENTS

Illustrations follow page 88

PEGGY GUGGENHEIM

The Angel of the City

I begin to see Peggy Guggenheim as the last of
Henry James's transatlantic heroines, Daisy Miller
with rather more balls.
—Gore Vidal

THE PEGGY Guggenheim Collection is visible from the
water, from the private boats, and from the *vaporetto*, the public
ferry that crisscrosses the Grand Canal on its serpentine course
through Venice. The museum is located in the Palazzo Venier
dei Leoni, a palace that was begun in the eighteenth century
and left unfinished, its construction interrupted some decades
before the Napoleonic Wars. The white building, with its stone
façade, is arresting, partly because it has only one story and is
so unlike the tall, elaborate Gothic, Renaissance, and Baroque
palazzi that line the Canal, and partly because something about
its spare, slightly severe elegance makes it a bit difficult to place

in time. Is it eighteenth century, neoclassical, or modern? An ancient Roman temple with a hint of the 1950s ranch house?

For thirty years it was where Peggy Guggenheim lived and where she installed one of the world's greatest collections of modern art—and it is where that art has remained since her death in 1979. Among the artists represented in the collection that she began to assemble long before the significance and value of their work was widely or fully recognized are Picasso, Pollock, Brancusi, Arp, Braque, Calder, de Kooning, Rothko, Duchamp, Ernst, Giacometti, Kandinsky, Klee, Léger, Magritte, Miró, Mondrian, Man Ray, Henry Moore, and Francis Bacon.

It was Peggy's decision to place Marino Marini's 1948 bronze *The Angel of the City* (*L'Angelo della Città*) at the entrance to her home, front and center on the landing facing the Grand Canal and nearly impossible not to notice if one is passing by boat. The bronze statue depicts a heavily simplified and abstracted horse and rider, reminiscent of Etruscan sculpture. The horse's neck and head are more or less parallel to the ground. The rider's body rises from the horse, at a right angle. His arms are outstretched and flung open wide, his head tipped back, as if in ecstasy. His body is arched, his phallus erect. The statue's most striking visual elements are: horse, rider, penis— specifically, a penis pointed at the traffic, the boats and passengers traveling between the museum, and, on the other side of the Grand Canal, the massive Palazzo Corner, which serves as the headquarters of the prefect of Venice. In her memoir, Peggy claims that Marini fashioned the statue so that the phallus was removable and that she detached it when she knew that nuns might be passing by.

There were many works of sculpture that Peggy could have chosen for the landing, and it says something about her nature —her ironic, playful, *lifelong* desire to shock—that she selected this particular piece of modern art with which to amuse or confront the officials and citizens of Venice. Peggy's mentor and adviser, the art critic and historian Sir Herbert Read, described the statue's placement as a challenge to the prefect.

Peggy claimed that the best view of it was in profile, from her living room, where she liked to sit and observe visitors reacting to Marini's work. What also makes the gesture so characteristic of Peggy are the contradictions and the ambivalence it expresses, the particular mixture of affection and provocation: Venice was, after all, a city that she deeply loved.

Out of This Century

In 1946 Peggy Guggenheim published *Out of This Century*, a wry and revealing account of her life so far. She was forty-eight years old. In New York, her avant-garde museum-gallery, Art of This Century, was a critical and popular success. Opened in October 1942, the innovatively designed exhibition space on West 57th Street had become a gathering place for the most important artists then working in New York, a showcase for exiled European émigrés and talented young American painters.

One of Peggy's assistants, Marius Bewley, noted who came to the gallery, how often, and for how long: Breton ("around a great deal"); Tanguy ("often"); Fernand Léger, Ossip Zadkine, and Marc Chagall; Matta, Pavel Tchelitchew ("was there a lot"); Duchamp ("frequently"); Man Ray ("once or twice"); Barr ("frequently"); Kiesler, Alexander Calder ("all the time"); James Johnson Sweeney ("would stay all day"); Motherwell, Jean-Paul Sartre . . . Pollock, Gypsy Rose Lee, David Hare,

Clyfford Still, Herbert Read ("spent a lot of time"); Mary Mc-
Carthy ("occasionally"); and so on.

Art of This Century, itself an example of what would later
be called installation art, remained a cultural force in New
York (and the wider world) from 1942 until 1947. At the gallery, viewers could study masterpieces such as Brancusi's *Bird in
Space*, works that might possibly have survived without Peggy's
intervention, but which she had rescued—along with many examples of what the Nazis termed "degenerate art"—from Europe on the brink of World War II. At Peggy's gallery, one
could contemplate the work of the Surrealists in a setting that
was livelier and more exciting than any existing museum or exhibition space.

Peggy was neither the first nor the only person to introduce Surrealism to the United States; there had already been
shows at the Museum of Modern Art and at private galleries.
But she was very good at making sure that it was talked about
by critics and seen by younger artists. She encouraged and
showed the work of a new generation of Americans, and it is
partly thanks to Peggy that American artists shook off the influence of Europe. One can only speculate about how different
the history of modern art would have been had Peggy not commissioned Jackson Pollock to paint a mural for the hallway of
her East Side apartment—a work that helped change the ways
in which Pollock and his peers thought about painting.

By 1944, when Peggy's friend the art critic Clement Greenberg began urging her to write her memoir, the gallery no longer required her constant presence, as it had at the start. Her
marriage to Max Ernst had ended the previous year, when he'd
left her for the painter Dorothea Tanning. Peggy was living
in a brownstone on East 61st Street with a wealthy British art
collector, Kenneth Macpherson, a homosexual with whom she
was having a complicated and disappointing love affair. Her
penchant for brief, casual erotic entanglements had taken on

a frenetic edge, and she had reason to be concerned about her daughter Pegeen, whose unhappiness and instability were becoming increasingly obvious and who had gotten into trouble in Mexico, from which she had had to be rescued by her father. Peggy was also disturbed and depressed by the war, and by the news from Europe, where she had spent much of her adult life, and which, as an American Jew in Nazi-occupied France, she had been forced to leave.

Encouraged by Greenberg, who had interested Dial Press in Peggy's book, and by her first husband, Laurence Vail, who was himself a writer and who agreed to help edit the manuscript, Peggy began serious work on the project while staying at the Cherry Grove Hotel, on Fire Island, in the summer of 1944. The literary critic Marius Bewley, who worked as Peggy's receptionist and assistant at Art of This Century, recalls her writing, propped up in bed, three sentences to a page. When she returned from vacation, she brought to the gallery, every morning, notepaper on which she'd written, in green ink, the previous night.

Peggy wrote to Laurence Vail, saying that her work on the memoir not only allowed her to forget the war but that it was currently more interesting than the gallery, which had become a "bore." She promised (or threatened) to write a book so honest that Laurence would never forgive her, and she added, "I've written 3,400 words since eleven today." In a letter to her friend the diarist and novelist Emily Coleman—who, on the strength of Peggy's journals, had long considered her to be a gifted writer—Peggy reported that she lived and breathed for her book. Interviewed in *Time* magazine after her memoir was published, Peggy remarked that it was more fun writing than being a woman—a statement that would have come as no surprise to readers of her memoir, who could compare the unhappy saga of Peggy's bad luck in love with the book's jaunty, confident tone.

It was Vail who suggested that she call her book *Out of*

This Century, a vast improvement over Peggy's original idea: "Five Husbands and Some Other Men." Peggy's title would have guaranteed that her memoir would be taken even less seriously than it was. Yet it would have revealed something about her character at that moment in her life: her tendency to define herself and to base her sense of importance, self-worth, and identity on the men with whom she was involved. Though Peggy always claimed that she never meant her memoir to be shocking but merely honest, there is something purposefully provocative about a title that is essentially a boast about her broad sexual experience, much of it with famous men.

As she wrote each chapter, Peggy gave the pages to Greenberg and Vail for their comments and edits. She also consulted the British art collector Dwight Ripley and the Anglo-Irish short story writer James Stern. Warned by Dial Press lawyers about the possibility of libel suits, she changed the name of some, though not all, of her relatives, lovers, and friends, giving them transparent pseudonyms that barely cloaked their true identities. Laurence Vail became Florenz Dale, his second wife, Kay Boyle, became Ray Soil, the painter Dorothea Tanning became Annacia Tinning. But Max Ernst remained Max Ernst, and Peggy's portrait of him—self-serving, faithless, and cruel—is one of the harshest in the novel.

Clearly, Peggy was still smarting from the pain of their separation, and her literary revenge disturbed Ernst. Max's son Jimmy, who had been Peggy's close friend, confidant, secretary, and gallery assistant, was horrified. In his own memoir, *A Not-So-Still Life*, Jimmy Ernst recalls the argument that erupted after Peggy showed him the chapter about his father and told him that Max should consider himself lucky that she hadn't been more explicit:

> I was appalled by its devastating pettiness and I could not believe that she could let such vindictiveness stand. Barely

avoiding vulgarity, it seemed almost an act of self-flagellation in its frequent failure of rational thinking. It was tailor-made for the scandal press and it would hurt her almost as much as the intended subject of destruction, my father. . . . Peggy and I did not see each other for a long time after that.

Jimmy's fears, at least about the response of the press, turned out to be prescient. When it was published in March 1946, *Out of This Century* received reviews that ranged from the negative to the venomous, a critical reception that might well have discouraged another author from ever writing again—anyone, that is, except Peggy, who by then had developed the defensive persona of a woman with the odd gift of seeming puzzled and even amused by slights and insults that others would have found intolerable.

Time found the "all-too-frank" memoir to be "as flat and witless as a harmonica rendition of the Liebestod, but it does furnish a few peeks—between boudoir blackouts—at some of the men who make art a mystery." In the *New York Times*, in a review headlined "Mechante—and de Trop," E. V. Winebaum objected to Peggy's "activities, worthy of tabloid headlines and recounted in tabloid prose" and to the "singular lack of grace and wit" with which she recounts her "world's series of love affairs" and her "long parade of amours." Ultimately, Winebaum threw up his hands at the task of decoding Peggy's motives. "It is useless to wonder what stimulates a well-known woman to write a book like this. . . . To be shocked is to fall into the trap laid so carefully and knowingly by the author." The *Chicago Tribune* proposed *Out of My Head* as a more descriptive title for Peggy's compendium of "nymphomaniacal revelations." Writing in *The Nation*, Elizabeth Hardwick lamented its "astonishing lack of sensibility," its "limited vocabulary," its "primitive style," and called the book "an unconsciously comic imitation of a first-grade reader."

Peggy's friends and associates were more encouraging. Fred Licht, the former curator of the Guggenheim collection in Venice, wrote that her books "are not to be read—as they have been read by most of her reviewers—as the confessions of a rich and wayward woman eager to shock people with the number and variety of her lovers. They are instead conversations with friends she can trust to understand. . . . The tempo of her prose, the asides, the sprinkling of anecdotes transmit with great precision her conversational tone and rhythm. . . . But above all, her autobiographies are exercises in self-irony and self-surprise."

The *New Yorker* contributor Janet Flanner, who published excellent essays on European culture and politics under the name of Genet, echoed Licht's opinion of "the book that I recall as a kind of annal of her emotional private life which, just as I had prophesied it would be, had been regarded as scandalous. Her detachment in looking back on life struck me as remarkable and in its way quite admirable. I felt she was telling the truth." And Gore Vidal remarked, "What I really liked about Peggy was her writing. I admire her style which was unaffected but effective. She was almost as good as Gertrude Stein. High praise. And a lot funnier."

Despite its *succès de scandale*, the memoir sold poorly and was not reprinted. Though it was rumored that the Guggenheim family had paid teams of messengers and scouts to buy up the entire first edition—a rumor that Peggy helped spread—there is no evidence that this occurred.

By 1959, more than a decade after her book's original publication, Peggy had closed Art of This Century and left New York for Venice, where she had displayed her collection at the 1948 Venice Biennale, a groundbreaking and controversial show that had introduced American Abstract Expressionism to

Europe. She had come to take herself, her career, and her legacy more seriously. And she began to reconsider the version of her life that had so outraged critics and readers.

She produced another edition of her memoir, *Confessions of an Art Addict*, a condensed and bowdlerized version that focused on her art-world career and omitted the more sordid details of her love life. She restored the real names of nearly all of the principal characters but merely summarized or suggested the dramatic events surrounding the ends of her marriages to Laurence Vail and Max Ernst.

In revising the book, Peggy couldn't bring herself to excise some of the passages that others had found to be what today might be called *inappropriate* ("The day Hitler walked into Norway, I walked into Léger's studio and bought a wonderful 1919 painting from him for one thousand dollars. He never got over the fact that I should be buying paintings on such a day.") But she did edit out her accounts of casual affairs and painful romantic betrayals.

Twenty years later, she looked back over the two extant versions of her life and decided, "I seem to have written the first book as an uninhibited woman and the second one as a lady who was trying to establish her place in the history of modern art. That is perhaps why the two books read so differently." Consequently, she resolved to make yet another attempt at telling her life story.

Again called *Out of This Century* and published in 1979, the year of Peggy's death, the third volume reads like the work of an uninhibited woman who had already established her place in art history. The scandalous revelations of the first edition have been restored, along with the real names of nearly all of her friends and enemies and the details of the insults and romantic perfidies that Peggy endured. There is an additional (and rather beautiful) section that covers her final years in Venice and brings the narrative up to date.

By that time, Peggy Guggenheim appears to have ceased caring about raised eyebrows or hurt feelings—and stopped wanting to raise eyebrows and hurt feelings. Rather, she was interested in compiling as complete and honest a record of her life as she could—or in any event, in telling her side of the story. In some cases, she does seem to have chosen the entertaining anecdote over the true one. She informs her readers that, after weeks of being unable to work, Jackson Pollock painted the mural she installed in the hallway of her apartment on East 61st Street in only three hours—when in fact it took a great deal longer and involved a substantial amount of deliberation and revision.

Despite Marius Bewley's prediction that *Out of This Century* would eventually be hailed as a "kind of classic in literary as well as artistic circles," it has never been widely read, nor has its artfulness been much recognized. And yet it is fully as well crafted, as original, and as engaging as *Nightwood*, the celebrated modernist novel that Peggy's friend Djuna Barnes wrote mostly during the summer when she and Peggy lived together in the British countryside. Though Peggy has been accused of exaggerating, scrambling chronology, and playing fast and loose with the facts, the truth is that her memoir is more amusing and incisive than much of what has been written about her, during her life and after her death.

Out of This Century is a remarkable document. It is hard to think of an important visual artist from the first half of the twentieth century who does not appear in its pages, in the company of an impressive number of celebrated novelists, memoirists, and poets. Yet the autobiography is far more than a rich and well-connected woman's annotated guestbook.

Peggy's style is highly conversational and deceptively offhand. Her readers may feel that an eccentric and extremely funny woman is speaking directly to them about her life—saying whatever comes into her mind, digressing whenever she pleases, and showing absolutely no concern for how her remarks (or her actions) will be interpreted and judged.

It is a memoir that begins with its author announcing, "I have absolutely no memory." Its somewhat dithery and girlish style, at once mannered and natural, vaguely resembles (insofar as it resembles anything at all) the wise-child narrative voice of *Two Serious Ladies*, the peculiar and brilliant novel that Jane Bowles (a friend of Peggy's) published in 1943. In her book, Peggy tells a story about leaving her house in search of adventure and wandering into a bar whose customers turn out to be gangsters. Peggy tells the gangsters she is a governess in New Rochelle, and they want to drive her home, but she's afraid and escapes them. Readers of *Two Serious Ladies* will notice at once how closely this incident resembles something that happens to one of Jane Bowles's heroines, Christina Goering. In fact, it's highly possible that Peggy, who read avidly and widely, was inspired and influenced by her friend's novel, which was published roughly a year before Peggy devoted herself to her literary project.

The photographer Roloff Beny has suggested that Peggy's prose style was strongly affected by Italo Svevo's *Confessions of Zeno*. She was introduced to Svevo's work by the British writer John Ferrar Holms, whom Peggy considered to have been the love of her life. And Peggy knew a great many writers: James Joyce, Samuel Beckett, and Mary McCarthy are among the most well known.

Even today, when the tell-all memoir and reality TV have raised the bar for candid self-exposure, much of what Peggy Guggenheim says still seems fresh and daring. However much she insisted that she had no desire to shock, it's hard not to be taken aback by passages such as this description of an abortion: "I had had an operation performed in a convent by a wonderful Russian doctor called Popoff. The nuns were strict and dirty and had no idea why I was there. . . . Dr. Popoff, who was supposed to have been the *accoucheur* of the Grand Duchesses of Russia, admitted one to the convent for a *curettage*, and then was credited for saying suddenly, in the middle of the operation: '*Tiens, tiens, cette femme est enceinte.*'" What makes the passage so unsettling is not merely the fact that Peggy is telling us this (even now, women are often reluctant to discuss having terminated a pregnancy) but, again, her tone—as if this doubtless painful and frightening operation had been a humorous escapade.

Peggy Guggenheim seems to have been born with, or developed early, the urge to unnerve, and this impulse or compulsion would serve her well as she devoted her life to showing art that was truly new and sometimes disturbing. Her idiosyncratic combination of outspokenness and reserve, of shyness and a craving for attention helped her broker the match between the world of twentieth-century art and the world of glamour, gossip, and media publicity. For better or worse, for better *and* worse, her tendency to mythologize herself and the artists she represented helped shape the contemporary art world, to turn artists into celebrities and socialites into art collectors.

Not long after the first version of *Out of This Century* was published, Herbert Read, who was one of Peggy's most influential advisers and whom she venerated and called Papa, wrote her a letter describing his response to her book:

> You have outrivaled Rousseau and Casanova, so who am I to criticize *Out of This Century*? I found it quite fascinating as a document—an historical document—and it is only the lack of introspective self-analysis which prevents it from being a human, psychological document (masterpiece?) like Djuna Barnes's *Nightwood*. That is why it is nearer to Casanova than to Rousseau—you are destined to be called the Female Casanova! It is perhaps even more amoral than Casanova, who, if my memory is not deceiving me, has some sniveling moments of self-disgust, or self-pity.

Leaving aside the tactlessness of comparing Peggy nega-
tively to Barnes (with whom Peggy had a stormy friendship,
and with whom she had felt competitive, as she did with many
of her friends) and the barely veiled insult of praising the Female Casanova for being more amoral than the male original, Read was wrong about the book lacking a psychological
dimension. It is in fact an incisive self-portrait, at once calcula-
tedly exhibitionistic and unintentionally revealing.

One can hardly fail to register the force of Peggy's wish to
be outrageous, but what is less immediately apparent is the fact
that her "natural" and candid tone is at least partly the voice of
a persona that she assumed over decades, a public face she adopted and which over time became indistinguishable from her
authentic self, as so frequently happens. The capricious and
slightly daffy ingénue we encounter in the pages of her book,
and whom one was likely to have met during her life, was only
a partial representation of the intelligent, determined woman
who worked hard and overcame any number of obstacles (not
least, the prejudice against women that then, as now, prevailed
in the art world) to run galleries, build her collection, fund worthy political causes, and support a long and remarkable list of
artists and writers. It is also clear that Peggy decided, early on,
that complaint and self-pity were dull and burdensome to one's
self and to others, and that she would do everything possible to
avoid portraying herself as a victim: easily hurt or fragile.

The more we learn about Peggy's life, the easier it becomes
to see how much of this painstakingly constructed persona was a
response to the perceptions of the friends and lovers who made
no secret of the fact that they thought of her as homely, unin-
telligent, promiscuous, miserly, politically naïve, self-involved,
and considerably more wealthy than in fact she was. She could
be difficult and petty about money, especially when she felt she
was being exploited. And her son and daughter, Sindbad and
Pegeen, had good reason to feel that she was an only intermit-

tently attentive mother. But she was also loyal, generous, brave, passionate about art, at once humble and savvy about seeking the counsel of (and learning from) advisers who knew more than she did. According to the artist Matta, "Peggy chose her friends and listened to them rather than to Merrill Lynch."

Peggy's younger sister, Hazel Guggenheim McKinley, recalled that when she asked Peggy to sign a catalogue of the 1969 exhibition of her collection then on view at the Solomon R. Guggenheim Museum, Peggy wrote, "To Hazel, who paints, from her sister, who writes and collects." Peggy Guggenheim thought of herself as both a writer and a collector, as indeed she was. Her memoir offers a portrait of a fascinatingly complex person, which is why, in the pages that follow, I have often tried to let Peggy have the last word—a policy which, one can safely assume, is what she would have wanted.

June 1941

MARSEILLES. JUNE 1941. A group has met for dinner and drinks, especially drinks, in a café in the French port city. Under normal circumstances, considering the cast of characters, their thorny entanglements, their shifting loyalties and antagonisms, and the dramatic scenes they had staged in the past, the atmosphere would have been tense. But the circumstances were anything but normal.

A year had passed since the Germans had invaded France. It was almost too late to escape the Nazi Occupation, and nearly all the guests at the dinner desperately needed to get out of Europe. Anxiety so intensified their usual volatility that it was only a matter of time before the sophisticated little party erupted in mayhem and violence.

Among the guests were two famous artists, Marcel Duchamp and Max Ernst. Accompanying Duchamp was Mary Reynolds, a beautiful heiress and war widow who had been Duchamp's lover for decades and who (alone among the American expatriates gathered that night) had decided to stay in Europe and work with the French Resistance.

Max Ernst was there with Peggy Guggenheim, the American heiress who had begun to establish herself as a serious art collector, dealer, and patron of modern art. Since 1938 she had run a popular London gallery, Guggenheim Jeune, which she had closed in advance of the coming war. Almost forty, she had only recently found a way to turn her interest in art and artists into a profession, a means of channeling her money, connections, and privilege into work she valued and enjoyed, a job that admitted her to a world which few women were permitted to enter unless they were great beauties, which Peggy Guggenheim was not.

In her twenties, she had read the art criticism of Bernard Berenson and toured Europe, applying his theories to the masterpieces of Renaissance painting. But during the subsequent decades her attention had been claimed by the demands of an unhappy marriage, the birth of two children, the death of a lover, tempestuous romances, family tragedy, all-night parties, massive amounts of drinking, periods of intense travel interrupted by interludes during which she established and oversaw large bohemian households in Paris, in London, and in rural beauty spots in England and France.

Though not as wealthy as some of her Guggenheim relatives, Peggy had enough money to live more or less as she pleased, though her desire for freedom (particularly sexual freedom) had long been at odds with her need to have an intense romantic connection with a husband or serious lover, no matter how marred by conflict, how unpleasant or even abusive that relationship might be. Even her friendships were turbulent. Throughout her life, Peggy maintained a large number of close female friendships that were as heady, emotionally demanding—and time-consuming—as love affairs. Among these friends were writers—Djuna Barnes, Mary McCarthy, Emma Goldman, Emily Coleman, and Antonia White—and art-world figures including Nellie van Doesburg and the art critic Jean Connolly. Despite the evidence of these powerful connections, Peggy was ambivalent about other women, claiming in her memoir, "I don't like women very much, and usually prefer to be with homosexuals if not with men. Women are so boring."

Though Guggenheim Jeune had transformed the London art scene and enhanced the reputations of many European painters and sculptors, it had never turned a profit. According to Peggy, it lost six thousand dollars during its first year. But Peggy's custom of buying work from every artist she exhibited had helped build her private collection, and by the spring of 1941 she had come to think of herself as something more than a socialite, an heiress, and an art-world hostess.

Just when she'd discovered that dealing and collecting art could give her a sense of purpose and the courage to be independent, the forces of history had sent her to Marseilles. There she had fallen madly in love with Max Ernst, the German Surrealist known for his phantasmagoric paintings of birds, for his beautiful young girlfriends, and for his irresistible personal charm.

Peggy and Ernst had met briefly at his studio in Paris. And they'd renewed their acquaintance in Marseilles, where Ernst was staying at Air-Bel, the mansion in which the American journalist Varian Fry, head of the International Emergency Rescue Committee, was housing the refugee artists whom he was helping to escape. With the encouragement of Eleanor Roosevelt, John Dos Passos, and Upton Sinclair, Fry had arrived in France with a briefcase containing three thousand dollars and a list of two hundred people—artists, scientists, writers, musicians, and film directors—who were considered to be in danger and who needed to leave Europe before they could be arrested by the Nazis. Assisted by a heroic staff, and gifted with prodigious creativity and personal courage, Fry, a sort of Surrealists' Schindler, eventually succeeded in saving more than a thousand people.

Four years before, the Nazis had exhibited in Munich a show of so-called degenerate art. Among the paintings on display were works by Klee, Kandinsky, Nolde, and Chagall; their non-German colleagues—Picasso, Matisse, and Mondrian, among others—were denounced in absentia. It was clear to modern European artists that their work, and perhaps their safety, might be in jeopardy if the Germans won the war. Max Ernst had already been twice interned as an "undesirable foreigner" in French detention camps, then imprisoned again by the Nazis as a traitor to the German people.

In early April 1941, Ernst invited Peggy to his fiftieth-birthday dinner at a black-market restaurant in Marseilles. At the party, when Max asked when they could meet again, Peggy had seduced him with the direct, effective—if not exactly subtle—line one can imagine her using on the men with whom she'd had affairs, a list that included Samuel Beckett, Yves Tanguy, and Jean Arp.

"Tomorrow at four at the Café de la Paix," she told Ernst, "and you know why."

Their romance had begun as a fling. But Peggy soon became infatuated with the man whom the art historian Rosamond Bernier has described as looking "like a cross between a noble bird of prey and a fallen archangel." Though initially intrigued by the sexually liberated, art-collecting American heiress, Ernst was not in love. His taste ran to women who, unlike Peggy, were very young and extremely pretty. He had made it clear that he was still obsessed with the beautiful painter Leonora Carrington, who, during Ernst's second internment, had gone mad, set free her pet eagle, sold their house for a bottle of brandy, and vanished into a Spanish mental asylum to which she'd been committed by her influential British family.

However much Peggy adored Ernst, she didn't hesitate to insult, alienate, and provoke him by offering him a flat sum— two thousand dollars, minus the price of his passage to the United States—for all his early work and for the right to pick whatever new work she chose. Using her money to exert her power and to punish men for not treating her well or loving her enough was a self-defeating pattern of behavior that Peggy had followed and would continue to follow in her dealings with her lovers.

In contrast to her volatile and unclear relationship with Ernst, Peggy's friendship with Marcel Duchamp was simple and rewarding. Peggy respected Duchamp, as did the contemporaries and peers on whom he exerted an enormous personal and esthetic influence. She had bought his work, and he had introduced her to artists and helped her decide what to show at Guggenheim Jeune. In her memoir, Peggy credits Duchamp with teaching her everything she knew about modern art. Throughout much of her career, Duchamp continued to be one of Peggy's most valued advisers.

Also present at the dinner was Laurence Vail, Peggy's former husband, a charismatic French-born American, a playwright, novelist, and painter. Though his moment as a golden boy had begun to fade, Vail had enjoyed a long run as the so-called King of Bohemia in Greenwich Village and among the American expatriates in Paris. With Laurence Vail was his second wife, Kay Boyle, an American novelist and short story writer who hated Peggy and whom Peggy despised. The two women—mother and stepmother—were ferociously competitive over the affections of Sindbad and Pegeen, Peggy and Laurence's son and daughter.

The children's lives were regulated by the complex custody arrangements specified in Peggy and Laurence's divorce, but these provisions had frequently been modified to suit their parents' whims and convenience, and the frequently changing exigencies of the grown-ups' feuds, love affairs, and travel plans. Pegeen lived with Peggy, Sindbad remained with his father and spent sixty days a year with Peggy. A great deal of time and energy was spent transporting the children between house-holds, though from an early age, they'd been allowed to travel by themselves from Peggy's homes in London and the British countryside to Laurence's in France.

Peggy's six-year marriage to Vail, begun in 1922, had rap-idly devolved from "thrilling" to "often too thrilling." Vail had enjoyed public displays of insult and humiliation. He picked fights with strangers and wound up in jail, but his most bit-ter altercations were with Peggy. He liked throwing her shoes out the window, smashing her possessions, breaking furniture, mirrors, and chandeliers, and knocking her down in the street. On one occasion he held her under water in the tub until she thought she was going to drown; once, when she was pregnant, he tossed a plate of beans in her lap; several times he threw her to the floor and walked back and forth on her stomach. A team of psychologists would be required to decode Laurence's pas-sion for rubbing jam in his beloved's hair while others watched. Peggy had endured Laurence's violence for years until her friends persuaded her that Vail was becoming a threat to her and the children.

Now he'd arrived at the Marseilles dinner already in a rage because Kay Boyle had abandoned him and gone to live in Cassis with her new lover, an Austrian baron named Joseph Franckenstein; now she needed Laurence and Peggy to help her get out of Europe. Kay had left Vail with six children— Sindbad and Pegeen; Kay's daughter Sharon; and the three daughters (Apple, Kathe, and Clover) whom Laurence and Kay had together—and the job of packing up their villa in Megève, in the Rhône-Alpes, where Vail had indulged his love of moun-tain-climbing and skiing.

The evening in the café in the port of Marseilles featured a convergence of historical and sexual tension, slightly ramped up by the presence of a professional art handler, René Lefèbvre-Foinet, who, with his brother Maurice, had helped Peggy pack and ship her art collection to New York. Peggy and the Lefèbvre-Foinet brothers knew that the art was in danger, that a collection belonging to an American Jew was at high risk of being seized by the Nazis. Peggy and René had become lovers until she had unceremoniously dumped him for Max Ernst. Now René had come to the dinner in Marseilles with a prostitute from Grenoble.

Even in the Unoccupied Zone, controlled by the collaborationist Vichy government, the situation for Jews, foreign nationals, and "degenerate artists" had become more risky. According to the treaty ending the brief "phony" war with France, Germany could extradite anyone the Nazis wished to have deported: Jews, Communists, Czechs, Poles, Germans, homosexuals, and antifascist intellectuals. In the autumn of 1940, the Vichy government had begun to pass increasingly harsh and restrictive anti-Jewish regulations modeled after the Nuremberg laws that had deprived the German Jews of their citizenship, their livelihood, and their most basic human rights.

One of the last escape routes led from Marseilles across Spain and Portugal to Lisbon, and from there to the United States. Long a hub for illegal commerce, Marseilles had become a center for black-market traffic, espionage, and desperate refugees, "a paradise for intriguers."

Peggy had bought tickets for Ernst, Vail, Boyle, and the six children to fly from Lisbon to New York on the luxurious Pan Am Clipper, one of the earliest commercial transatlantic flights. She had also overseen the vast quantities of paperwork required to obtain exit permits, entry permits, transit visas to cross the Iberian countries, and permission (for Ernst) to enter the United States. Peggy's own visa had expired, and in a characteristic gesture combining a rich person's entitlement with flighty impulsivity, she'd changed the expiration date herself. Laurence didn't have a visa, and Max's U.S. entry permit had run out and had to be renewed. Long lines formed in front of the American consulate in Marseilles, queues that Peggy cut with Max by flashing her U.S. passport. The subject of emigration and the legal formalities involved was very much in the air of Marseilles, and consumed much of the time and energy of Varian Fry's Emergency Rescue Committee, to which Peggy had donated generously. Peggy gave the committee 500,000 francs and may have given Fry more in secret. It was precisely the sort of obligation—the manifestation of noblesse oblige—that she had been raised to fulfill.

In Marseilles, an order for the arrest of foreign Jews had been issued, and Peggy had already had a close call that she describes in her memoir:

> At this time all Jews were being combed out of the hotels in Marseilles and were being sent to live in special places. Max told me not to admit that I was Jewish, if the police came to question me, but that I should insist I was an American. It was a good thing he had warned me, because early one morning after he had left and the breakfast cups were still on the table, one of the police arrived in plain clothes.

Eager to find out how Peggy stayed out of prison, we might read rapidly on. Or we may pause and wonder, What is wrong with this passage?

Obviously, the Jews in Marseilles were being combed out of plenty of places beside hotels. Peggy Guggenheim was the one in the luxury suite. And what were these "special places" to which Jews were being sent? By the time Peggy wrote the first version of her memoir, the fate of Europe's Jews was widely known. Was "special places" one of the "humorous" and intentionally provocative turns of phrase that no one but Peggy seemed to think was funny? Everywhere in her memoir one sees evidence of the desire to unnerve and startle that directed so many aspects of Peggy's life, from her racy conversational style to her fashion sense, her outré taste in jewelry and sunglasses, and, most important, her desire to show avant-garde art in an entirely new (and outrageous) setting.

But why did a woman who had gotten out of Paris just days before the Germans invaded and who had been donating so lavishly to Varian Fry's Emergency Rescue Committee need Max Ernst to warn her not to tell the police she was Jewish?

Peggy Guggenheim knew perfectly well that she was Jewish —and what that meant to the Germans. She had grown up in an insular society of wealthy German Jews who aspired to be like the aristocrats in Edith Wharton's New York novels, though presumably unlike the Jewish caricatures who populate Wharton's fiction. Peggy's lack of interest in formal religion is evidenced by the fact that she'd gotten into trouble with her mother for shopping for furniture on Yom Kippur. And yet she was delighted when a Jersey Shore hotel that banned Jews burned down. According to family legend, two of her male relatives died of broken hearts after being rejected because of their ethnicity; one had been turned away by a hotel, the other denied admission to a New York private club.

Both these events, which Peggy's memoir relates with spirited bemusement, were *causes célèbres* that reverberated through Jewish high society—and the country. When, in 1877, Peggy's great uncle Joseph Seligman was refused a room at Saratoga's Grand Union Hotel by its manager, Judge Henry Hilton, the snub ignited a scandal that made newspaper headlines. The affair sparked one of the first public conversations about antisemitism, a discussion continued when another of Peggy's uncles, Jesse Seligman, resigned from Manhattan's exclusive Union League Club after his son Theodore was denied admission. "Though he was still technically a member, Jesse never set foot inside the Union League Club again. His bitterness over the episode probably shortened his life, just as the affair with Judge Hilton shortened his brother's."

Peggy had a similar experience when, during World War I, she and her mother and sisters were permitted to stay overnight in a Vermont hotel with restrictive racial policies—but required to leave the next day. Peggy's comment—"This gave me a new inferiority complex"—is clearly intended, like so much else in her memoir, to be at least partly ironic. But the theme of her "inferiority complex"—a term that had come into common usage with the popularization of Freudian theory— was to recur throughout her life. Peggy's "complex" had many causes: she was Jewish, she believed she was ugly, and, perhaps most damaging, she was convinced that she was less intelligent and talented than her friends—who readily confirmed her view of herself as being "not smart enough."

Her lack of confidence—or, perhaps more accurate, her ambivalence about her self-worth—was such a well-known facet of her personality that Peggy could joke about it. When her friend Emily Coleman complimented Peggy for having no pretensions, Peggy replied, "I have pretensions to inferiority." During the summer of 1944, Peggy rented a house on the shore of a Connecticut lake "where Jews were not supposed to bathe." By then, the threat of exclusion no longer fed her sense of inferiority; instead, she took great delight in circumventing the restriction by sending her friend the composer and writer Paul Bowles to sign the lease for her. It amused her to be known by the locals, that summer, as Mrs. Bowles.

In many ways, Peggy Guggenheim prefigured a certain type of contemporary American Jew, one whose Jewish identity would have more to do with a simultaneously pained and defiant response to antisemitism than with a depth of personal and authentic feeling for Jewish religion or culture. The size of this group increased in the wake of the Holocaust's evidence of antisemitism's newest and most hideous mutation, and again whenever the state of Israel appeared to be in danger. Many years later, in Venice, Peggy refused to meet Ezra Pound because of the openly pro-fascist stand he had taken during World War II.

Like many people, Peggy was a creature of contradictions. The pleasure she took in the burning of the "restricted" hotel coexisted with a certain tolerance for the simultaneously off-hand and egregious antisemitism of 1920s Paris. In the chic expatriate society into which Peggy flung herself headlong, it was acceptable, even stylish, to say awful things about Jews.

Such conversations occur throughout Ernest Hemingway's novel of that period, *The Sun Also Rises*. Peggy's cousin Harold Loeb, who started a literary magazine named *Broom* and who moved to Paris to write, is said to have been the model for Robert Cohn, Hemingway's pretentious, cowardly Jew. Hemingway's hero, Jakes Barnes, is initially friendly toward Cohn despite his "hard, Jewish, stubborn, streak." Later, in the grip of sexual rivalry, Jake is less sympathetic. His friends remark that though Lady Brett has gone off with lots of men, they "weren't ever Jews." They criticize Cohn's "Jewish superiority" and warn Brett that if she goes about "with Jews and bullfighters and such people, she must expect trouble."

In an unpublished memoir, Laurence Vail's name for his wife was Pigeon Peggenheim. His novel *Murder! Murder!* is punctuated with antisemitic asides, and nearly every argument between the narrator and his money-obsessed, penny-pinching Jewish wife devolves into a volley of insults directed at the Jewish people. Kay Boyle seems to have shared her husband's prejudices. By the time Peggy and the Vails met for dinner in Marseilles in 1941, Laurence and Kay had visited Austria, where they'd been enchanted by Nazism and where Kay described one of Hitler's radio addresses as "really moving."

William Gerhardie's novel *Of Mortal Love*, in which Peggy and her lover John Holms appear as characters, features a visit to a restaurant owned by an "oily Italian Jew." And Peggy's close friend Emily Coleman remarks, in her diary, that being born a woman is like being born a Jew: one has to do everything twice as well to achieve any recognition.

Later in the diary, Coleman is less tolerant and sympathetic: "Like all the rich [Peggy] likes to support someone who accepts what she gives and never asks for more. She knows they always *will* ask for more. . . . What is galling is being in the power of people who have no right to be in power over you . . . Although she half feels this (a phenomenon for any person born with money), the other half is close wicked Jewish, careful of the disposal of every cent."

Peggy must have learned to disassociate herself from her friends' (and her first husband's) jokes and from the acceptable clichés. Still there is a disturbing story about Sindbad visiting his mother after his parents' separation, when Laurence Vail and Kay Boyle were (or so Peggy believed) trying their hardest to turn the children against her. The communal household in which Peggy lived in the British countryside during the summers of 1932–33 was fond of games, and when Peggy jokingly asked Sindbad whether he knew how to play the Guggenheim game, he asked, "What's that? Swindling people?"

Peggy herself harbored conflicting feelings about other Jews. At the Wailing Wall, on a trip to the Middle East not long after Sindbad was born, Peggy had reacted to the sight of the religious at prayer much as some of her German-Jewish relatives on New York's Upper East Side had responded to the wave of immigrants who arrived from the shtetls of eastern Europe at the start of the twentieth century. "The nauseating sight of my compatriots publicly groaning and moaning and going into physical contortions was more than I could bear, and I was glad to leave the Jews again." But Peggy was smart enough to comprehend that no amount of special pleading—surely the Germans realized that she was not like *those other Jews*—would dissuade the Gestapo if they decided to arrest her.

Ultimately, Peggy Guggenheim needed, or claims to have needed, Max Ernst to warn her not to tell the police she was Jewish not because she was insufficiently aware of this fact and its potential consequences, but for the same reason she'd needed Laurence Vail to teach her about Europe, wine, food, art—and life. Even though she had begun a business—and a career—of her own, she still believed that she required a man to make certain essential decisions and translate reality into terms she could understand. "I was inexperienced when I met [Laurence] and I felt like an awful baby in his (what I considered at the time) sophisticated world. . . . He brought me into an entirely new world and taught me a completely new way of life."

Though Peggy had been frightened by the prospect of the coming war, she was determined to test her luck and had stayed in Paris, buying art, until a few days before the Nazis occupied the city. It was Laurence Vail who had finally determined that they should go to America. "I did not know what to do about the future," Peggy recalled. "But Laurence kept very calm and decided everything for me."

From 1928 to 1934 Peggy had required Vail's successor and her great love, John Ferrar Holms, to teach her about poetry, philosophy, and the pleasures of literary conversation. And when she began collecting and showing art in the galleries she opened in London and New York, she had needed, and would continue to need, a succession of advisers beginning with Marcel Duchamp—and all but one of them male—to tell her what she was looking at, and looking for.

Though she had her own money and her own ideas about how to spend that money, though she had her own ambitions and friendships, she had been raised and socialized to take direction from a man. She lived in an era and a milieu in which women needed men to explain the world to them, to decide what was important; women were expected to manage the household and raise the children, or to supervise the servants who did. Without a man to direct her, without the rewards of male attention and the validation of male desire, a woman was a deficient, an incomplete—a failed human being. This traditional view of gender roles and power relations is all the more striking given that Peggy and so many of the women she knew saw themselves as rebels warring against convention and tradition.

It was, Peggy writes, a good thing that Max Ernst had warned her about what to conceal from the police. Because the detective who came to her hotel room was suspicious. When he noticed that the date on Peggy's travel permit had been crudely altered, she insisted that the officials in Grenoble had changed it. Then he asked why she wasn't registered in Marseilles. What most alarmed Peggy was the fact that she had, hidden in her room, large quantities of the illegal black-market currency needed to finance everyone's passage home.

The policeman asked whether her name was Jewish, and she replied, No, her grandfather was Swiss, from Saint-Gallen. True, he was Swiss, though of course it was also true that she was Jewish. The officer had never heard of Saint-Gallen and began to search the room. Peggy said he wouldn't find any hidden Jews in the cupboard or under the bed—at which point the agent ordered her to follow him to the police station.

Gallantly, he left the room so that Peggy could dress. Meanwhile she tried to figure out how to hide the black-market currency and leave a note telling Laurence and Max where she'd gone. Waiting for Peggy in the lobby, the detective happened to meet one of his superiors, who had a soft spot for Americans, perhaps because of the large shipload of food that the United States had recently sent to ease the shortages in France. When Peggy came downstairs, she sweetly asked the senior officer how to get to the police station so she could register. He was very happy to give mademoiselle directions.

Later when she complained to the landlady about the detective, the woman said, "Oh that is nothing, Madam, they
were just rounding up the Jews."

After a sobering paragraph about the frequency with which
Ernst encountered the "new society" of ghostlike men he knew
from the concentration camps in which he'd been imprisoned,
Peggy slips back into the more comfortable persona of the
dizzy rich girl, writing that Max spoke of the camps "as casu-
ally as if he was referring to St. Moritz or Deauville or Kitzbuhl
or some other equally well-known resort." This fear of letting
the mood get dark is a sort of tic in the memoir, as it apparently
was in Peggy's conversation.

At the Marseilles café, Peggy and her friends drank to keep
their minds off the dangers they were facing. But the more they
drank, and the later the hour grew, the harder it became to
avoid reopening the wounds they had inflicted on one another
in the past.

Kay Boyle detonated the first of the evening's explosions
by nonchalantly mentioning that she'd heard some bad news:
the boat transporting Peggy's art collection from Europe to
New York had sunk somewhere in the Atlantic.

Peggy and Kay's rivalry over the children's love and loyalty
was aggravated by Kay's belief that Peggy resented the money
Kay earned from her writing because it helped support her
family and thus reduced their dependence on Peggy. More recently, Kay's anger had spiked when Peggy refused to finance
the escape of Kay's lover, Baron Franckenstein. Now that the
Austrian aristocrat was safely en route to the United States,
Kay's rage had subsided, but still she couldn't resist tormenting
Peggy by fabricating a rumor about the loss of her paintings
and sculptures.

It was among the cruelest lies that Kay Boyle could have
told. Peggy's father, Benjamin Guggenheim, had died in the

wreck of the *Titanic*, so to raise the specter of another maritime disaster was particularly appalling. And Peggy would have been devastated by the ruin of the collection in which she'd invested so much time, energy, and money, a project that, she had begun to understand, would be her life's work. Peggy's detractors claimed that she cared more about her paintings than she did about her son and daughter, and she fueled the unpleasant gossip by referring to her paintings as her children and to the refugee artists whose work she showed in her gallery as her "war babies." Indeed she had a deep, almost maternal feeling for the art she owned; for Peggy collecting was not an investment strategy but a passion.

When, on the eve of the German invasion, it had become obvious that her collection could not safely remain in Paris, Fernand Léger (in whose studio Peggy had been shopping for art on the day of the Norwegian invasion) suggested that the Louvre might agree to let Peggy use a fraction of the rural hiding place where the museum was sheltering its holdings. The museum directors said they were sorry, but the work that Peggy was asking them to safeguard was too modern to merit saving.

"What they considered not worth saving were a Kandinsky, several Klees and Picabias, a Cubist Braque, a Gris, a Léger, a Gleizes, a Marcoussis, a Delaunay, two Futurists, a Severini, a Balla, a Van Doesburg, and a 'De Stijl' Mondrian." Also considered not worth saving were paintings by Miró, Max Ernst, de Chirico, Tanguy, Dalí, and Magritte. And the museum refused even to consider helping Peggy preserve the sculptures by Brancusi, Lipschitz, Giacometti, Moore, and Arp.

However disturbing and shortsighted, the museum's decision serves as a useful reminder that the art Peggy owned was still far from being widely recognized as significant—or even as art. And it obliges us to remember what has been obscured by the recognition these artists later achieved: how avant-garde

Peggy's taste was, and how much daring she showed in championing work that France's most venerable museum considered unworthy of hiding along with its Poussins and Chardins.

Of the approximately 150 works en route to New York, many had been bought just before and after the invasion, when Peggy had been, she claimed, on a mission to buy a picture a day. Accompanied by her friend and adviser Howard Putzel, she had embarked on a manic spree that took her to the studios and galleries of the most celebrated artists and dealers in Paris. Other artists brought her work they hoped to sell, early in the morning, when she was still in bed.

After the Louvre refused its help, Peggy arranged to have the collection hidden in a barn near Vichy, on the grounds of a château to which her friend Maria Jolas had evacuated her bilingual school for children; Jolas had understood that because Peggy was Jewish, it was essential to get her collection out of the Occupied Zone.

Days before the Germans entered Paris, Peggy left the city with another friend, Nellie van Doesburg, in the Talbot sedan powered by the gasoline that Peggy had been hoarding on the balcony of her apartment. Eventually, they reached Megève, where Peggy was reunited with her son and daughter, and where (after renting a house on the Lac d'Annecy) she spent the summer having her hair dyed different colors to provide a cover for her secret love affair with the hairdresser.

But the collection was still in jeopardy. Dispatched from Vichy to the railway station at Annecy, it had stayed on a station platform under a leaking ceiling and protected only by tarpaulins. A friend proposed that Peggy send the work to the Musée de Grenoble, whose director agreed to store it. But sensibly concerned about how the Vichy officials might respond to a show of degenerate art, the museum director was unwilling to exhibit it, as Peggy would have liked.

In any case, storing the work at the Grenoble Museum failed to solve the problem of what to do with it when Peggy left for the United States. René Lefèbvre-Foinet, Peggy's shipping agent, had suggested that the art be packed and shipped along with Peggy's household linens, books, pots and pans, and other personal effects—a task made somewhat less arduous when Peggy and René became lovers. Accompanied by the prostitute from Grenoble, René was present when Kay Boyle announced that the collection was lost; he too must have been distressed to learn that his work had come to nothing.

Nor was this good news to Marcel Duchamp. Better connected than the others, Duchamp had arranged for his own exit from Europe. By posing as a buyer for a cheese store, he had managed to make numerous trips in and out of the Unoccupied Zone, smuggling in materials that he planned to use in making fifty or so constructions—his boxes—when he arrived in the United States. And he had packed the materials with the art and household items in Peggy's shipping containers.

Even now it is awful to contemplate the images that Kay Boyle's little joke evokes. Brancusi's *Bird in Space* shedding its shroud of blankets, the gleaming bronze spinning until it fell to the ocean floor. Arp's *Shell and Head* and Giacometti's *Woman with Her Throat Cut* plummeting amid the naval wreckage. Kandinsky's *Dominant Curve*, Braque's *The Clarinet*, Léger's *Men in the City*, and Dalí's *The Birth of Liquid Desires* spreading along the surface of the water. Or the photographs of Man Ray and Berenice Abbot buckling, slicked with salt.

Had Peggy's collection been lost at sea, many Americans might never have seen some of the greatest works of art created in Europe before the war. Had it been lost at sea, we would have been denied an essential piece to the puzzle of what European painters and sculptors had accomplished during that critical period. Had it been lost at sea, the Abstract Expressionists might never have had the chance to study the art that would so strongly influence their work—and which they would eventually react against.

To imagine what would have been lost is to acknowledge what was saved, and by extension the importance of what Peggy Guggenheim accomplished.

Eventually, Kay Boyle admitted that she'd been joking. "She loved to imagine things like this," Peggy commented drily.

The party calmed down long enough for Laurence Vail to remember *his* grievance: Kay's desertion and her refusal to help him and their children pack up their home in Megève.

Vail's marriage to Kay Boyle had been considerably less rancorous than his life with Peggy. Unlike Peggy, Kay refused to let him rub jam in her hair, and like most bullies, he had backed down. It was agreed that Kay was better at "handling" Laurence, mainly because she had learned to throw a preemptive tantrum whenever she sensed one of his coming on. It was too bad, Peggy's mother had said, that Laurence hadn't been as scared of Peggy as he was of Kay.

But that night Laurence's fury frightened even his normally intrepid wife. When Kay stood, explaining that she had to leave, Vail knocked the glasses off the table and began throwing crockery around the café. Then he lifted the marble tabletop and threatened to smash it down on Kay's head.

Duchamp stepped between them, restraining Vail while Kay rushed out of the café. Kay was to recall running down the street with tears streaming down her face, flanked by Duchamp on one side and Vail on the other. When Duchamp advised Kay to go to his hotel room, where she would be safe, Vail threatened to kill them both.

Finally, the couple agreed to go to Peggy's room and try to work things out. Lying on separate beds, Laurence and Kay reached an agreement about the care of the children and how they would arrange their lives in the United States. At some point during the night, the Gestapo knocked on the door, but the Germans left when Laurence and Kay produced their U.S. passports.

And so ended a night that, however dramatic, was by no means atypical of Peggy Guggenheim's evenings at that time in her life. Later, she would call "such wild, fighting parties *charmantes soirées*." Passions were incited and indulged, friendships tested, deepened, or terminated, shocks and insults administered and received, while a historical crisis transpired, just slightly offstage. Tensions boiled over into violence, a temporary accord was reached, the fates of the children were decided in ways that seemed the least likely to inconvenience their parents. And meanwhile Peggy Guggenheim's art collection sailed on, making its steady and peaceful journey from Europe to New York.

---◆◆◆---

Her Money

WHENEVER PEGGY Guggenheim is mentioned, by those who knew her and by those who have written about her after her death, among the motifs that recur most often are her money and her nose. What connects these two seemingly disparate entities are the clichés of antisemitism, the shorthand with which bigots signify Jews and Jewish identity. That is what Jews care about and how one identifies them: their money, their noses.

In Peggy's case, these two nouns and their distasteful implications signified the ways in which she saw herself and was viewed by others: as a wealthy woman with the bad luck to be physically unattractive, thanks to what Peggy, her family, and friends saw as her disfiguring flaw—an overly large nose. In fact, photos of Peggy as a young woman show her to be quite pretty, not a striking beauty, but appealing nonetheless. And that appeal continued well into middle age, when she disfigured herself by dyeing her hair a harsh unflattering black and painting her mouth an equally unlovely and strident scarlet.

In Venice, some of her earlier prettiness returned when, in her final decades, she resolved to dress more elegantly and decided to let her hair go gray. Though it is said that she never let herself be photographed in profile, a few portraits taken from that angle do exist; her nose is hardly what one would call pert, but it's by no means the bulbous monstrosity that she—and others—have suggested that she had.

In any case, these topics—her nose, her money—so thoroughly dominate the contemporary and posthumous conversations about Peggy Guggenheim's life that we have to consider them, separately and together, and to look at how they formed her character, how they enabled her to do what she did, to have the adventures she wished to have, and at the same time cut off other avenues that might have led her to seek very different sorts of fulfillment.

In the privileged society in which Peggy grew up, the Jewish families who acquired mansions in New York's best neighborhoods and on the Jersey shore dressed in the latest fashions, served elaborate meals on the finest china, with elegant silver and crystal, and hired servants to do whatever they felt was beneath them. A Guggenheim, or a Straus, or a Seligman was expected to be meticulously well mannered and to avoid anything that might be considered ostentatious or vulgar. "Whenever Meyer Guggenheim [the patriarch of the Guggenheim family and Peggy's grandfather] took his sleigh or carriage through the park, he drove alone, managing the reins himself, avoiding the showiness of a coachman and footmen. There was almost a rule of thumb: the richer one was, the more decorous and inconspicuous one endeavored to be."

It was assumed that the families in the Guggenheims' circle would donate to worthy causes because it was a sort of Eleventh Commandment, to "give back"—to show gratitude to the country that had enabled them to prosper, and to honor the God whose mysterious blessing had obligated them to look out for the welfare of those less gifted or lucky. This tradition would inspire Peggy's relatives to lend their names to a museum and a foundation. And it would move Peggy to respond to charitable requests, to support friends whose work she believed in, and to help a group of artist-refugees to escape Europe during the war.

However much Peggy might have preferred to maintain some privacy about the depth of her pockets, the terms of her inheritance, and her eccentric and impulsive vacillations between generosity and miserliness, that dignity was denied her. Her friends speculated at length about how rich she was. Was it true, as she often insisted, that her inheritance required her to survive on an income that, while generous, had limits? Was she wealthy by ordinary—or by Guggenheim—standards?

What's clear is that she was always the richest member of her circle, the one who paid the rent on the homes that she and a revolving cast of artists and bohemians inhabited in Europe and in New York, the one who was expected to pick up the check after dinner. In a letter to his father, the writer Charles Henri Ford describes a night out in Paris, a lavish meal followed by drinks at several nightclubs and ending with Peggy "having paid for the whole party." In John Glassco's *Memoirs of Montparnasse*, a couple based on Peggy and Laurence Vail treat the author and his friends to "oysters, langoustines with mayonnaise, sweetbreads and green peas, parsley potatoes, a pineapple tart, and a magnum of champagne," after which "the waiter presented the bill with a discreet murmur. Would Madame sign?"

Many people who knew Peggy, even tangentially, were quick to ask her for money. A lover of Emily Coleman's, an Italian named Bianchetti, was perpetually suggesting ways in which Emily might borrow or extort funds from her prosperous friend. Regardless of what Peggy claimed about the state of her bank account, the mention of her family name conjured up (as it continues to do today) the image of more money than one person, even Peggy, could spend in a lifetime. "Peggy is so clumsy with money," Coleman wrote, "because it is so important to her."

Long before Peggy established herself as a patron of the arts and as the nexus of a changing coterie of dependents, the history of her family fortune was well known. As a boy, her maternal grandfather, James Seligman, had demonstrated a flair for business in his mother's dry goods shop in the Bavarian town of Baiersdorf. In 1837 her great-uncle Joseph, then seventeen, emigrated to the United States. Arriving in rural Pennsylvania, where he had relatives, Joseph worked first as a clerk, then as a peddler, selling household goods door to door.

Soon he was able to bring his siblings over from Germany, and they opened a series of stores across the country and ultimately in San Francisco, where they arrived in time for the Gold Rush and began to trade in the precious metal. During the Civil War, they secured government contracts to manufacture military uniforms. By the time the war ended, they were not only rich but had established themselves as bankers: respected members of New York's upper class.

The family's new social prominence and respectability did not preclude the operation (exacerbated by the inbreeding common in the insular Jewish community) of what appears to have been a rogue gene that produced, in the Seligmans, aberrant behaviors ranging from the simply peculiar to the self-destructive and tragic. Peggy took a perverse familial pride in her relatives' odd habits and delusions. During his divorce from Peggy, Laurence Vail threatened to sue for full custody of their two children by claiming that Peggy was as unbalanced as the rest of her family. Fortunately, he never acted on his threat, for the evidence of hereditary instability might have proved persuasive.

Her grandmother, her mother, several aunts and uncles, and Peggy herself were obsessed with cleanliness and phobic about germs. One uncle bathed several times daily, another refused to shake hands; the women (again including Peggy) compulsively wiped down household surfaces and sprayed the air with Lysol. Peggy's obese Aunt Adelaide conducted a love affair with an imaginary pharmacist named Balch. Uncle Washington survived on a diet of ice and charcoal, wore jackets with zinc-lined pockets, and killed himself at fifty-six. Two cousins were also suicides; one shot his wife and then himself. Her pathologically miserly Uncle Eugene was known for arriving precisely at dinnertime and assuring his relatives' welcome by performing a trick that involved moving the dining room chairs together and wriggling across the seats on his belly, like a snake.

Peggy's mother, Florette, suffered from a disorder that made her repeat everything three times, and, like Eugene, from the intermittent, irrational stinginess of which Peggy was also accused. On family trips, Florette tipped the hotel porters so poorly that the busboys marked her valises with X's, and took every opportunity to drop and damage them.

At twenty, Peggy suffered a nervous collapse; among her symptoms was a compulsion to pick up burned matches from the street out of terror that they might start a fire. And when, in 1928, Hazel's sons died in a fall from a high building in Manhattan, Hazel was believed to have killed them.

Despite their history of minor eccentricity and madness, the Seligmans looked down on Peggy's paternal relations, the Guggenheims, who had arrived in New York later than the Seligmans and who had rapidly made their fortunes in commerce and mining rather than in the more refined pursuits of banking and finance.

In 1847 Simon Guggenheim, together with his wife and seven children, left Switzerland for Philadelphia. His twenty-year-old son Meyer became a peddler, applying his innate ingenuity to developing new products that would improve on ones that existed. His first success involved a superior stove polish he concocted with a chemist friend. He prospered in the lace and embroidery business until, in the 1880s, Meyer—by now the middle-aged father of seven sons—invested in lead and copper mines in Colorado, and in the machinery to pump out the water that had made the mines inoperable. Over the next twenty years, the Guggenheims acquired smelters and refineries, formed an exploration company that led to the purchase of gold, tin, copper, silver, and diamond mines in Africa and Latin America—and became one of the wealthiest families in the United States.

As profitable as the business was, it failed to hold the interest of Benjamin, Meyer's handsome fifth son, who ceased working with his father and brothers in 1901. Seven years earlier, he had married Florette Seligman, a union that that Seligmans considered "a *mésalliance*." To explain that she was marrying into the well-known mining family, the Seligmans sent a cable to their relatives in Europe saying, "Florette engaged Guggenheim smelter." This became a cherished family joke, as the message that actually arrived had been mistakenly transcribed as, "Guggenheim smelt her."

Florette and Benjamin's first daughter, Benita, arrived in 1895. Three years later, on August 26, Marguerite (known first as Maggie and subsequently as Peggy) was born. Hazel, their youngest, followed in 1903.

Peggy was an infant when Benjamin moved his family to a grand limestone mansion on East 72nd Street, a home that Peggy would recall as a place of unmitigated gloom and bad taste. In the marble entrance hall was a stuffed eagle that Benjamin had shot (illegally) in the Adirondacks, a sort of companion piece to the bear rug—with a tongue that fell out and teeth that came loose—in the mirrored Louise XVI parlor. In an upstairs reception room, beneath a tapestry of Alexander the Great entering Rome, Florette invited "the most boring ladies of the haute Jewish bourgeoisie" to weekly tea parties that her reluctant daughter was forced to attend.

It's not clear when Benjamin Guggenheim was first unfaithful to his wife, but another family story suggests that womanizing was a character flaw rather than his response to an unsatisfactory marriage: Benjamin is supposed to have told a nephew, "Never make love before breakfast. One, it's tiring. Two, you may meet someone else during the day that you like better." By the time Peggy was five or six, everyone seemed to know that her father had lovers; the first of these may have been a nurse who was hired to massage his head and soothe the pain of his neuralgia.

Years later Peggy confided in her friend Emily Coleman that, from the age of ten, she knew that her father had mistresses. ("At twenty," Coleman comments wryly, "I had never heard of a mistress.") One of the most telling incidents of Peggy's childhood occurred when she was seven. In her memoir, she describes hiding under the grand piano and weeping because her father had banished her from the table for saying, "Papa, you must have a mistress as you stay out so many nights." What's striking is the child's impulse not only to confront her father with the truth but, in doing so, to shock the grown-ups.

This desire to observe the effects of excessive frankness continued to influence Peggy's social style. She conducted candid discussions about sex in her children's presence, interrogated her dinner guests about their romances, embarrassed acquaintances with descriptions of her own erotic exploits—conversations in which one can hear echoes of Benjamin's salacious advice to his nephew. And her attraction to the shocking was to be reflected in her determination to show the sort of art that would have appalled the people who attended Florette's afternoon teas.

Relegated to the care of nannies by her often-absent father and her distracted mother, Peggy craved attention and discovered that being outspoken was one way to obtain it. As an adult, she told Emily Coleman that she liked to know that people were talking about her, even if she knew they were saying cruel things.

The Guggenheims' troubled marriage contributed to the misery of Peggy's childhood, "one long protracted agony" of which she claimed to have had "no pleasant memories of any kind." Early on, she was drawn into Florette's domestic war with Benjamin, whom Peggy so adored that she would race to greet him when, on returning home, he would whistle a tune he had composed to "lure" her downstairs. Though she blamed her parents for involving her in their problems—a situation that, she claimed, made her "precocious," by which she appears to have meant sexually precocious—she was to repeat this mistake in her own married life, encouraging her children to take sides in her battles with Laurence Vail and Kay Boyle.

When Peggy was thirteen, her father "more or less freed himself from us." He began spending more time in Paris, where he lost much of his fortune, investing in a company that proposed to install elevators in the Eiffel Tower. According to Peggy's accountant, Bernard Reis, she would have inherited approximately $200 million if her father had chosen to remain with the family business instead of branching out on his own.

In the spring of 1912, Benjamin Guggenheim booked passage back to New York on a steamship that was kept in dry dock by a worker's strike. Determined to get home in time for Hazel's birthday, he bought tickets—for himself, his secretary-valet, his driver, and (though this is in some dispute) his mistress—on the RMS *Titanic*. According to the ship's steward who brought the bad news to Florette, Benjamin and his secretary refused the offer of life preservers when the ship was going down. Dressed in formal evening clothes, they helped their fellow passengers into lifeboats.

Peggy claimed never to have recovered from the loss of her father. For the rest of her life, she wrote, she would look for a man to replace him. Decades removed from childhood tragedy, she was able to speak of it ironically, thus providing the punchline for this passage from the British painter Michael Wishart's memoir, *High Diver*. "My friendship with Peggy has been punctuated by mishaps. We have been trapped together, suspended in a small wire cage which was a lift described by Cocteau as dating from a time before lifts were invented and once, during a violent tempest, we were in a small boat aimed at Capri, which turned backwards somersaults while attempting to enter the haven of Sorrento. Peggy's father had drowned on the *Titanic* and she thought it would have been unkind of Fate to dispose of two generations in the same fashion."

Benjamin's death had immediate repercussions for her family. Once it became clear that he had lost millions on his Parisian business ventures, the Guggenheim uncles convened to decide how to maintain Florette and the girls in something approaching the style to which they had been accustomed. When Florette realized that her brothers-in-law had shielded her from the truth, she sold some of her jewels and furs and moved her daughters to more modest quarters.

Not long afterward, Peggy's maternal grandfather, James Seligman, died, leaving Florette with a substantial inheritance. And in 1919, when Peggy turned twenty-one, she received $450,000—which would translate, today, to approximately $5 million. Her uncles suggested that she keep her money in trust and live off the income, which amounted to more than $20,000 a year—again representing a tenth of what that sum would mean today. When Florette died in 1937, Peggy inherited another $450,000. And so we return to the question of how much money Peggy Guggenheim had.

She was rich compared to most people, but in fact *not* wealthy by Guggenheim standards, and her resources were meager compared to the fortune her family had enjoyed and spent freely when she was a child. Yet her friends assumed that she had unlimited funds, and that the attempts at economy with which Peggy tempered her generosity betrayed a selfish and miserly nature. Since no one (including Peggy, it seems) knew precisely how much she was worth, speculations about her income varied wildly.

Memoirs of Montparnasse includes a scene in which Peggy and Laurence Vail appear under the names of Sally and Terence Marr, and which begins with a discussion of Sally's finances:

> "Money," [Bob] said, "is not so important as Fitzgerald thinks, but you have to have some. Not too much, though. You'll notice this when we have lunch with Sally and Terence Marr tomorrow. . . . Wonderful people, and they'd be perfectly happy if only she didn't have so goddamn much money."
>
> "How much does she have?" asked Graeme.
>
> "Twenty, thirty million, how do I know? I bet she doesn't know herself."

In William Gerhardie's *Mortal Love*, Peggy appears as Molly, "a rich American." "[She] was indeed rich, but complained of recent curtailments in the source of her income: to which Walter and Dinah listened with the pained surprise of the poor told that the rich are also poor."

In 1931 Charles Henri Ford reported to his father, "Djuna [Barnes] and I were taken to dinner the other night by Peggy Guggenheim, a millionairess: she has 30 million dollars in her own name, and will have 70 million when her mother dies. . . ."

When we got home, Djuna said, would you think just looking at her that she had 70 million dollars?"

Djuna Barnes was one of the people who benefited most (indeed, for much of her life) from Peggy's generosity—and who grumbled bitterly about her stinginess. From the 1920s on, Peggy sent Barnes a monthly stipend, ceasing only temporarily when Djuna exhausted her patience or when Peggy felt it would be more helpful for Barnes to try to survive on her own. She sent her former teacher, Lucille Kohn, "countless $100s." She lent Berenice Abbot the money to buy a camera, gave the poet Margaret Anderson five hundred dollars to publish the *Little Review* (which serialized James Joyce's *Ulysses*), raised funds to enable the anarchist Emma Goldman to write her autobiography, paid for Emma's friend Margaret Fitzgerald to travel to Europe for her health, and sent an annual sum to the indigent widow of Peggy's lover, John Ferrar Holms.

In 1925 Peggy financed the opening of a shop in Paris to showcase the highly original lampshades made by her friend the poet Mina Loy; the store also sold underwear and hosted an exhibition of Laurence's paintings. Though the boutique on the rue du Colisée failed, it represented Peggy's first attempt to exhibit and sell art.

During the German occupation, Peggy donated enough money to get André Breton and his family out of France, and she supported Max Ernst long after they arrived in the United States. Years after their divorce, she continued sending an allowance to Laurence Vail, and when Robert McAlmon, a friend from her Paris days, fell ill with tuberculosis, she wrote him a monthly check. These, of course, were direct contributions, given without any expectation of repayment or compensation. An even greater fraction of her inheritance was spent supporting painters and sculptors by buying their work.

Yet everyone seemed to have a story about her penny-pinching, her awkward (but not unreasonable) insistence on adding up the checks that arrived at the end of the meals to which she treated her friends. Early in her friendship with Djuna Barnes, she made the writer the odd gift of some old, much darned lingerie, a present that Barnes found insulting but which she nonetheless wore when she wrote.

The character based on Peggy in *Memoirs of Montparnasse* bargains hard to reduce the price of the tickets to a pornographic film to which she and her companions have been invited. Years later friends would complain that, at her parties in Manhattan, she served only potato chips and cheap whiskey that she secretly decanted into empty bottles of single malt. A home-cooked dinner at Peggy's might feature a course of Campbell's canned tomato soup. An assistant who worked for her in Venice recalls being told that she was permitted to serve customers a glass of vermouth—but only *after* the customers had agreed to buy a painting.

The barbed critique of her parsimony would continue after her death, most egregiously in Anton Gill's 2003 biography, *Art Lover:* "Peggy enjoyed being the mistress of the first real home she had ever had in her own right, and promptly began to annoy Laurence with her habit of keeping precise, even anal, household accounts. No centime could be left unaccounted for, and no groceries went unremarked. It wasn't simply stinginess: Peggy enjoyed accountancy, and a sense of the value of money was in her blood." One hardly knows what to make of the oxymoronic phrase, "parsimonious benefactress," with which Andrew Field describes Peggy in his biography of Djuna Barnes. And in her biography of Jackson Pollock, Deborah Solomon refers to Peggy's "characteristic stinginess" and her "singular stinginess."

According to the art historian John Richardson, "Peggy was stingy. At her parties in Venice, she always served the cheapest Italian red wine that you could buy. And the food was awful. But I think she was saving her money to buy art. The rest didn't interest her much. She was stingy with her money—but generous with herself."

Clearly, there were times when Peggy used money to wield power in destructive ways. In a brief documentary film made during her old age, *L'Ultima Dogaressa*, a gardener who worked in her palazzo in Venice recalls her reluctance to pay him a fair wage. During her marriage to Laurence Vail, she clearly enjoyed telling him how much he could spend, and what he could spend it on. Perhaps the most damning account of her attempts to control others by withholding support concerns the composer John Cage, who, together with his wife, Xenia, was a houseguest at Peggy's Manhattan home in the early 1940s:

> The nastier side of Peggy's nature surfaced when she learned that Cage, who was virtually unknown at the time, was planning a concert of his percussion music at the Museum of Modern Art. Peggy wanted him to give a concert at the opening of her Art of This Century gallery in the fall, and she was so annoyed about the MOMA concert, which would precede her opening, that she canceled the one at her gallery and rescinded her offer to pay for Cage's percussion instruments from Chicago. She also informed Cage and Xenia that they would have to move out of Hale House. Stunned by this harsh news—he was literally penniless at the time—Cage retreated through the usual crowd of revelers until he came to a room that he thought was empty, where he broke down in tears. Someone else was there, though, sitting in a rocker and smoking a cigar. "It was Duchamp," Cage said. "He was by himself, and somehow his presence made me feel calmer." Although Cage could not recall what Duchamp said to him, he thought it had something to do with not depending on the Peggy Guggenheims of this world.

Peggy enjoyed toying with people, and she knew that the subject of money—her money—was one that could be counted on to discomfit, offend, and inspire gossip. Rosamond Bernier remembers attending an opening at the Art of This Century gallery. Peggy presented her with a catalogue, inscribed it with a personal note, and then demanded that Bernier pay her six dollars. A similar anecdote concerns a visit that Peggy's Aunt Irene made to the gallery, after which Irene too was expected to pay for her copy of the catalogue.

In her fair-minded and informative 2004 biography, *Mistress of Modernism*, Mary V. Dearborn tells a story about Peggy inviting friends for dinner at a restaurant in Venice and informing them that it would be her treat, an offer that (on the basis of gossip and perhaps experience) they distrusted. Consequently they ordered very little—and then were surprised and chastened when Peggy picked up the bill. Peggy frequently joked about money and about the fashionable outfits that her money allowed her to buy. When her friend the novelist Antonia White complimented her on her expensive rawhide bag, Peggy replied that Antonia must not know her very well, because the bag wasn't rawhide; it had cost five shillings. Soon after, when White remarked on a pretty scarf Peggy was wearing, Peggy said, "This—I use it for a dust-cloth."

In London, in 1936, after an argument over whether Peggy would pay for Djuna Barnes's passage back to the United States, Peggy told Emily Coleman that "her finances were in a bad state and she worried about it; she gives so much money away that she has very little left. I almost wept, because I can't ever decide whether Peggy is a saint or the meanest person I have ever met—and neither can she. She actually gives away ¾ of her income, to a point where she is worried, sometimes, whether she has enough money to buy herself a dress."

Peggy's behavior suggests that she was often hurt by, impatient with, and resentful of friends who expected her to pay for everything and who then openly and (as she must have known) privately accused her of being ungenerous. One can sense in her actions the irritation of someone who feels that she is being taken advantage of, valued and (as seems to have been the case with Max Ernst, among others) loved only for her money. In her diary, Emily Coleman reports that Peggy's lover John Holms claimed that Peggy was unable to conceive of a friend as anyone but a person who wanted her money.

A touching passage in Peggy's memoir describes Laurence Vail confirming her worst fears: "Because of my money I enjoyed a certain superiority over Laurence and I used it in a dreadful way, by telling him it was mine and he couldn't have it to dispose of freely. To revenge himself he tried to increase my sense of inferiority. He told me that I was fortunate to be accepted in Bohemia and that, since all I had to offer was my money, I should lend it to the brilliant people I met and whom I was allowed to frequent."

Even now, the phrase—"allowed to frequent"—is distressing to read, and one hears in it the barely sublimated voice of Peggy's anxieties, fears that would be intensified when she left Vail for John Holms and lived among friends who agreed that Peggy was incapable of participating in, or even following, their scintillating conversation. If only she had been as brilliant and talented as the people who "allowed her" to enjoy their company, a closed circle to which, for women (with a few exceptions) beauty and money were the only keys.

Another of the observations made about Peggy Guggenheim is that she was remarkably unaffected by, and indeed oblivious to, the thoughtless and even cruel ways in which she was treated; she often endured slights and insults that would have crushed a more tender soul. According to John Richardson, "Peggy was pretty thick-skinned. Even, in a way, insensitive. If someone disliked her, she overlooked it. People said things to her . . . most people would never have spoken to them again. But Peggy seemed to accept this as her fate."

A rather different reading of Peggy's character appears in *A Not-So-Still Life*, a memoir by the painter Jimmy Ernst, who worked as Peggy's secretary after she returned to New York from Europe in 1941. To Jimmy, Peggy's shyness and lack of affectation "suggested a painful past. At the same time there were flashes of brilliance, charm, and a warmth that seemed to be in constant doubt of being reciprocated. It must have been the anticipation of such rejection that caused her abruptly changing moods, penetrating retorts and caustic snap judgments, but never at the cost of her femininity."

Her Nose

PEGGY'S OLDER sister Benita was considered to be the family beauty. And from an early age, Peggy thought of herself, and was encouraged to think of herself, as the homely one.

Not long after she came into the first installment of her inheritance, Peggy resolved to do something about her nose, which she believed she'd inherited from her father's family: the Guggenheim "potato nose." In her memoir, she tells the story much as she relates the other traumatic events in her life: as a joke. "In the winter of 1920, being very bored, I could think of nothing better to do than have an operation performed on my nose to change its shape. It was ugly, but after the operation it was undoubtedly worse."

In the same droll tone, she recounts the gruesome details. At the time, cosmetic surgery was such a new specialty that Peggy had to go to Cincinnati to find a doctor willing to perform a rhinoplasty. Asked to choose a new nose, Peggy opted for something poetic, a nose "tip-tilted like a flower," like one she had read about in Tennyson. Under local anesthetic and in great pain, Peggy heard the surgeon say that he couldn't complete the operation, and she told him to leave things as they were.

Subsequently, she adds, her nose functioned as a barometer, swelling up in bad weather. All her life, she would remain dissatisfied with her appearance, and in particular, with a nose that was hardly improved by decades of heavy drinking. Tellingly, she describes both Mary Reynolds and Djuna Barnes as having "the kind of nose I had gone all the way to Cincinnati for in vain." And she writes, with delight and gratitude, of her mother-in-law, Gertrude Mauran Vail, the first woman Peggy met who not only admired her looks but who thought she was prettier than Benita and Hazel. "I had been brought up to believe that I was ugly, because my sisters were great beauties. It had given me an inferiority complex."

Reading memoirs and social histories of this period, one gets the impression that it was heavily populated by "beauties," "great beauties," and "famous beauties," women like Nancy Cunard, Lady Diana Cooper, Luisa Casati, and Lorna Wishart, women who may have had other accomplishments, and interesting characters, but who were best known for their looks. In our day, even the prettiest women are more likely to be identified by what they do (supermodel, actress, socialite) than as "beauties," but in Peggy's times, these fortunate creatures were principally celebrated for their ability to attract, seduce, marry, and break the hearts of gifted, wealthy, or otherwise important men.

It was almost as if beauty were a viable (if short-lived) career for women, a profession to which Peggy believed she had been denied admission. Peggy first mentions her "inferiority complex" in connection with the hotel that turned her away because she was Jewish, and with the world of social and sexual opportunity from which she felt she was excluded because she was "ugly."

As so often happens, others intuited—and adopted—Peggy's low opinion of herself. A close friend of Peggy's daughter Pegeen told Mary Dearborn, "Maybe if she'd—I don't know, had a better nose job—that would have kept her from this fundamental insecurity."

Anton Gill relates with some relish the harsh appraisals of those who knew her: "In the thirties, Nigel Henderson, the son of her friend Wyn, said that she reminded him of W. C. Fields, and the same resemblance was called to mind by Gore Vidal decades later. The painter Theodoros Stamos said, 'She didn't have a nose—she had an eggplant,' and the artist Charles Seliger, otherwise full of sympathy and regard for Peggy, remembered that when he met her in the 1940s her nose was red, sore-looking, and sunburned: 'You could hardly imagine anyone wanting to go to bed with her, to put it cruelly.'"

In fact, Peggy boasted of having had more than four hundred lovers. If she couldn't be beautiful, she would compensate by being seductive, sexually liberated—and available. Like a number of her friends—especially Emily Coleman—she was preoccupied with sex, and seemed to thrive on dramatic and frequently violent scenes of intense jealousy and accusations of sexual betrayal.

"She was very plain," said Rosamond Bernier. "That accounted for her throwing herself into bed with so many men." There is perhaps no more accurate barometer of the sexual double standard than to compare the tone of such remarks with the admiration with which history has viewed physically unprepossessing men who had no trouble attracting beautiful women.

Philip Rylands, director of the Peggy Guggenheim Collection, offers a more charitable view of Peggy's love life. "I think one reason she may have had so many love affairs was that she was interested in people, she wanted to find out who they were."

Convinced that she was homely, Peggy would feel grateful to the men who (in her view) overlooked her appearance, fell in love, and took on the job of providing her with an education. This gratitude enabled her to endure a succession of psychologically (and physically) damaging relationships, but Peggy extracted payment by using her money to control and even humiliate the men who controlled, humiliated, and depended on her.

Education

ACCOUNTS OF Peggy Guggenheim's life, including her own, gloss over her early twenties, as if those years were merely a corridor between childhood and adulthood, a long wait in the harbor before her ship sailed for Europe. But in fact that period—spent mostly in New York, meeting people entirely unlike her family and her parents' friends—was formative.

Peggy was the sort of student who learned more from the world and from a succession of carefully chosen advisers than she did from her formal schooling, such as it was. Determined that his daughters be educated, her father sent the family on improving trips to Europe, where Florette visited her Seligman relatives and stayed at stylish hotels. The most memorable of the French governesses, Mrs. Hartman, introduced the girls to art, French history, nineteenth-century British novels, and the operas of Wagner, but Peggy was more interested in other things: at eleven, she had fallen in love with a friend of her father's, who disappointingly married someone else.

Peggy briefly attended the Jacoby School for Jewish Girls, but withdrew when she came down with a respiratory ailment. Even as she struggled to keep up with her courses, she developed a love for literature; she was to remain a lifelong reader, a fan of Proust and Henry James, whose novels about wealthy women courted by fortune-hunters and American innocents who fare badly in their dealings with cynical Old World sophisticates must have seemed like sympathetic representations of her own experience. In his novel, *Murder! Murder!* Laurence Vail describes the character based on Peggy trying to concentrate on a Dostoyevsky novel, which enrages the protagonist, who is attempting to read his own poetry out loud.

Returning to school, Peggy fared somewhat better and decided to go to college. But Benita, the adored older sister, dissuaded her, and Peggy decided not to continue with her formal education, a decision she always regretted. She studied with private teachers, one of whom, Lucille Kohn, was a political radical whom Peggy credited with being the first to suggest that one could break away from the gilded prison of shopping trips and debutante balls. And Kohn herself claims to have been the person who persuaded Peggy that people like the Guggenheims had an obligation to change the world for the better.

In 1918 Peggy made her first real attempt at independence —a wartime job that involved helping soldiers buy uniforms at reduced rates. Overworked, bored, and exhausted, she stopped eating and sleeping and eventually suffered the breakdown that involved her obsessively collecting burned matches. Her situation improved a year later, when she came into her inheritance and celebrated by taking a cross-country trip with a distant relative as her chaperone. A short-lived engagement to an aviator was broken off, to Peggy's distress, when she criticized the provincialism of his hometown, Chicago.

Newly recovered from her grueling encounter with plastic surgery, Peggy took a job at a dentist's office but soon found another position that would dramatically broaden her perspective. Two cousins, Harold Loeb and Marjorie Content, owned a bookstore called the Sunwise Turn, located across Vanderbilt Avenue from Grand Central Terminal.

One of its founders, Madge Jenison, recalled the question she asked herself, which led her to open the store. "Why doesn't some woman open a real bookshop . . . which would pick up all that is related to modern life in the currents that would flow in and out of the door of such a shop and make them available; and bring to it the tradition of a professional spirit which puts its knowledge and integrity at the disposal of the community, and what it does not know, finds out, as a physician does. I cannot remember just when it began to seem to me that a bookshop of a different kind must be opened in America, and opened at once, and opened by me."

What's striking is how closely Jenison's vision of her bookstore would be echoed, decades later, by the way Peggy spoke and wrote about her decision to found an art gallery in London and later in New York. "Of course," noted Jenison, "one of our advertising secrets was that we tried to make the shop a cult, something unlike other things, and offering one a breath of experience even to buy a book there." Again, this "secret" sounds very much like the reasoning behind the design and the "cultish" atmosphere of Peggy's galleries, Guggenheim Jeune and Art of This Century.

"In the winter of 1919–20," wrote Jenison, "we had eight unpaid apprentices—all women of a great deal of background. They sold thousands of dollars' worth of books for us. They filed invoices. They swept floors. They ran errands. Sometimes they did everything well. I have sometimes secreted a smile behind a monograph to see . . . Peggy Guggenheim, in a moleskin coat to her heels and lined with pink chiffon, going out for electric-light bulbs and tacks and pickup orders at the publishers, and returning with a package large enough to make any footman shudder and a careful statement of moneys disbursed."

What a revelation it must have been for Peggy, emerging from the claustrophobic, convention-bound world that her parents and their parents had constructed, to meet writers and artists who cared deeply about literature and art and gravitated to a bookshop that also functioned as a gallery and a performance space for poetry readings and plays. Though Peggy received no salary, she was permitted to buy books at a discount, and she voraciously read the modern classics. Cultural celebrities—Amy Lowell, Lytton Strachey, Marsden Hartley—passed through the Sunwise Turn, and when the customers encouraged Peggy to study art history, she immersed herself in the writings of Bernard Berenson.

She appears to have been headed for the career that would take her twenty years more to achieve, a vocation she might have followed earlier had she not been distracted by her compulsion to seek personal, sexual, and intellectual validation from the men whom she considered her teachers or (in her Freudian-inflected version) replacements for the beloved father, lost on the *Titanic*.

Among the people she met was a couple who, perhaps more than any of her new friends, changed her life: the publisher Leon Fleischman and his wife, Helen. They introduced her to Alfred Stieglitz—and, more important, to Laurence Vail.

Vail, then hoping to establish himself as a playwright, had long blond hair swept back from a striking aquiline profile, bright blue eyes, and an air of confidence and entitlement engendered by his popularity—and notoriety—in the café society of New York and Paris. Everywhere, Vail's arrival signaled that the party had started, and Peggy had never seen anyone like him.

He was about twenty-eight at this time, and to me he appeared like someone out of another world. He was the first man I knew who never wore a hat. His beautiful, streaky gold hair streamed all over as the wind caught it. I was shocked by his freedom but fascinated at the same time. . . . He was like a wild creature. He never seemed to care what people thought. I felt when I walked down the street with him that he might suddenly fly away—he had so little connection with ordinary behavior.

In 1920 Peggy returned to Europe, a different sort of traveler from the bored, sulky girl who had accompanied Florette to sip tea with relatives. Changed by the books she had read and by the people she'd met at the bookstore, she was in a "frenzy" to see great art. She knew where every important painting was located and insisted on seeing them all, even if it required an arduous detour to some distant country village. When a friend suggested that she would never understand Bernard Berenson's criticism, "I immediately bought and digested seven volumes of that great critic. After that I was forever going around looking for Berenson's seven points. If I could find a painting with tactile value I was thrilled."

In Paris, Leon and Helen Fleischman again brought Peggy together with Vail, who, with Leon's approval and encouragement, was having an affair with Helen. Peggy's second encounter with Laurence coincided with her decision that her virginity was an encumbrance from which she must free herself, at once.

Laurence was living with his mother, a New England aristocrat, and with his sister Clothilde, who looked like his twin and with whom he had a relationship so close that Peggy noted that they were "made for incest; and by not indulging in it they augmented their frustrated passion." He was eager to get away from his parents; Peggy was avid for sexual experience, and, after considerable awkwardness, she not only slept with Vail but startled him (as she tells it) by insisting on trying all the sexual positions she had seen in a book of erotic frescoes from Pompeii.

The start of their marriage was no less awkward. Laurence proposed to Peggy at the top of the Eiffel Tower but had second thoughts when she accepted; he fled the capital for Rouen, then returned to find Peggy's friends and family trying to talk her out of marrying him. It was agreed that he would travel to Capri, and that Peggy would go to New York to think it over. On the eve of their separate journeys, Laurence appeared at the door of Peggy's hotel room and persuaded her to marry him the next day, March 10, 1922, at the municipal office in the sixteenth arrondissement. On the way to the wedding, Laurence invited the tramps and prostitutes he passed to attend the ceremony.

The next morning, after a drunken celebration, Peggy was already regretting her decision: "As soon as I found myself married, I felt extremely let down." When Laurence had been uncertain about the marriage, Peggy was determined they marry. Now that I had achieved what I thought so desirable, I no longer valued it so much." A decade later, Peggy would say that she was never in love with Vail. "I just wanted fucking."

Peggy and Laurence set off on their honeymoon, stopping in Rome to assert their independence by looking up former lovers. Laurence rented a villa on Capri, where they were joined by Clothilde, whom Peggy termed "the thorn in my marriage." Fiercely possessive of her brother, Clothilde "always made me feel that I had stepped by mistake into a room that had long since been occupied by another tenant, and that I should either hide in a corner or back out politely."

After the honeymoon, the Vail siblings went off to the Basque Coast, and Peggy left to visit Benita. Back in New York, Peggy discovered that she was pregnant, and she returned to Europe. There (with remarkable calculation, given their commitment to bohemian spontaneity) she and Laurence decided that the child should be born in London so that, if they had a boy, their son would not be subject to French military conscription.

Peggy rented a house in Kensington, and after a raucous dinner party during which a guest threw a pillow at her and her water broke, the baby was born on May 15, 1923. Peggy and Laurence planned to name him Gawd, but common sense or human kindness prevailed, and they settled on Michael Cedric Sindbad Vail.

Sindbad was the name that Laurence preferred, and that was how their son would be known—until, in later years, his friends in Paris would call him Mike.

Among the more startling parts of Peggy's memoir—a section that now seems more extreme than her descriptions of the sexual exploits (and the abortions) that discomfited her contemporaries—is her account of her first marriage. In those years, spousal violence was not considered the problem it is today; many people, including Peggy's relatives and friends, witnessed Laurence's aggression and did nothing to intervene. Only when things got truly frightening did friends encourage Peggy to leave Vail—for another man.

Peggy's version of these events is echoed in books about her, and in others by and about her social circle, though John Glassco seems to have met Mr. and Mrs. Laurence Vail at a rare companionable moment. The litany of abuse that Peggy recites in her memoir reflects the sense of menace that pervades Vail's *Murder! Murder!* Even though his book is fiction, possibly composed under the influence of alcohol and of such proto-Goth literary models as Comte de Lautréamont's *Les Chants de Maldoror,* the novel is disturbing.

Its hero, Martin Asp, roams the city looking for women to murder. He may already have killed one, but he isn't sure. Occasionally he returns home for marathon fights with Polly, his grouchy, money-obsessed Jewish wife, and for visits from his mother-in-law, Flurrie, who shares with Florette Guggenheim the habit of repeating everything three times.

When Peggy claimed to have been offended by the character based on her in a draft of Laurence's "extremely funny" novel, he threw the manuscript into the fire and dictated a less hurtful version to a typist. It's hard to imagine a draft more odious than the one that survived and was published in 1931: "There was a certain quality about a Jewish argument about money which no Christian like Martin could possibly understand: he saw the sordid facts, the mean details, not the rich human emotion." Throughout the book are chilling antisemitic rants that seem to be coming from the author rather than his hero.

There is also a passage in which Martin nearly drowns Polly, a scene that corresponds to an event recorded in Peggy's memoir.

> Suddenly I hear hot water running. I see steam. I glance up. Polly has turned on the hot-water tap. I am very angry. Does she think I have thrown her into the bath to amuse herself?
>
> I rush to the bath edge. "Remember," I cry, "the story of the brides in the bath. Remember what Smith used to do to his wives?"
>
> I grasp her firmly by the hair, then push, push, push. And now neck, chin, lower lip, upper lip, nose, eyes, forehead gradually disappear. Suddenly—am I a weakling? A neurotic? Hamlet?—I let go. I kept on thinking of reasons why she should not die.

A caricature is a portrait of sorts, and beneath Vail's grotesque Polly, one catches a glimpse of Peggy, even though Martin describes her with nearly unmitigated contempt and scorn. Among the qualities he mocks is her impulse to donate to worthy causes, a remnant of the culture in which Peggy grew up and of her teacher, Lucille Kohn.

> It occurs to her that the Flat-Footed Footmen's Fund have repeatedly solicited her assistance. Shall she send a check to the F.F.F.F., or should she put the sum aside to help Martin out of his sordid scrape? . . . Suddenly she remembers she has neglected the Iowa Prison Reform Association for a whole year. She sits down, endorses an illegible cheque to the I.P.R.A.

In fact, Laurence Vail would be one of the principal beneficiaries of Peggy's noblesse oblige. Awarded three hundred dollars a month in their 1928 divorce settlement, he remained such a steadying and welcome presence in Peggy's life that she continued to send him money until his death in Paris, forty years after their marriage ended. When she returned to Europe in 1947 after closing her gallery in New York, she traveled to Capri with Vail and his third wife, Peggy's friend the art critic Jean Connolly.

Of the "Five Husbands and Some Other Men" about whom Peggy intended to write, Laurence Vail was the only one with whom she maintained a lasting connection. This was in part because he was the only one with whom she had children but also because, when sober, he was a source of good advice, an intermittently responsible parent who could rise to the occasion when his children were involved, and a substantial presence in the lives of the people around him.

Peggy showed Vail's work at Art of This Century and kept several of the wine bottles he decorated in her bedroom until she died. They vacationed together and shared homes with their new lovers and spouses. Peggy turned to Vail for advice on her marital problems, on the editing of her memoir, and on her fraught relationships with their son and daughter. Ultimately, it was Vail who persuaded her not to donate her collection to the

Tate Gallery in London but to keep it in Venice. Because his behavior was so erratic and his art less than brilliant, Laurence Vail
has been undervalued as one of Peggy's all-important advisers.

By the time Vail threw Peggy against a wall on New Year's
Eve, 1925, during a trip to Italy, she was pregnant again, this
time with her daughter Jezebel Marguerite "Pegeen" Vail, who
was born on August 18, a delivery hastened, Peggy believed, by
the plate of beans that Laurence threw at her. Once more they
left France to have the child, this time in Switzerland. Then
they returned to the south of France and moved into a former
inn where Jean Cocteau had stayed with his lover Raymond
Radiguet.

With two small children, a nanny, a cook, sheepdogs, ser-
vants, and a succession of houseguests, they led a vibrant domestic life, interrupted by trips to ski resorts and to Paris, and
by progressively more appalling scenes in which Laurence beat
Peggy and was arrested by the French police—not for spousal abuse but for endangering the other customers in a bar. A
New York Times article dated December 30, 1926, and headlined
"Love Lifts Jail Sentence of Laurence Vail When Frenchman
He Struck Wins His Sister" reports that "American dramatist"
Laurence Vail was sentenced to three months in prison for hit-
ting a certain Captain Allain Lemerdy over the head with a
champagne bottle in a Montparnasse cafe. The charges were
dropped when Lemerdy fell in love and decided to marry the
accused's sister, Clothilde.

In the summer of 1927, Peggy learned (by accidentally opening and reading a telegram addressed to Laurence, asking him to
gently give Peggy the bad news) that her sister Benita, whom
Peggy loved more than anyone, had died in childbirth. The
following October, even as Laurence's behavior was becoming
so distressing that Peggy's friends had begun advising her to

divorce him, another family tragedy distracted her from the trouble at home.

In New York, where Peggy's younger sister Hazel had gone from Paris on learning that her husband was divorcing her, Hazel's two young sons fell to their deaths from the terrace of a cousin's sixteenth-floor apartment.

The newspaper account recounts the events that led up to the tragedy but makes it hard to understand how the boys' deaths occurred: Hazel "was seated on a bench or on the low parapet with her back to the street. The younger boy was in her arms. Terence, jealous of his brother's favored spot in his mother's arms or anxious to see more of the view, was pushing and pulling, trying to climb into his mother's lap. In the scramble one of the children went over the edge. [Hazel] made an effort to catch him and the other child also fell." Nor does the item explain why the distraught mother failed to call for help until a neighbor telephoned the police. Though it was widely believed that Hazel had killed her sons, the boys' deaths were officially ruled to have been accidental; Hazel suffered a breakdown and was sent back to Europe to recover.

By then, Peggy had made up her mind to leave Laurence—a decision made easier by the fact that she was no longer facing life without a man. Peggy had fallen in love with the writer and critic John Holms and was being encouraged to divorce Vail by Emma Goldman, living nearby in Saint-Tropez.

Goldman's politics somewhat resembled those of Peggy's teacher Lucille Kohn; her influence, like Kohn's, would inspire Peggy to be braver than she was raised to be. Since her arrival in the United States from Russia in 1885, Goldman had earned a reputation as a political activist, a writer, a popular lecturer and labor organizer, a champion of women's rights, of equality for homosexuals, of birth control, and of social justice.

Emma seemed not to mind that Peggy came from a class at which she and her anarchist comrades had literally taken aim.

Goldman's lover, Alexander Berkman, had gone to prison for attempting to shoot the industrialist Henry Clay Frick, who moved in circles similar to those of the Guggenheims. By pure chance—his wife had injured her ankle—Frick had decided not to sail on the same *Titanic* voyage on which Peggy's father died. And today Frick's art collection is housed in a museum on Fifth Avenue, not far from the one that was started by Peggy's Uncle Solomon.

Deported from the United States in 1920 and disenchanted by the political climate in Russia and Germany, Emma Goldman had for some time been leading a peripatetic and uncertain existence. Friends had been urging her to write the colorful story of her career, and it was decided to take up a collection that would enable Goldman and Berkman (who had been released from prison) to survive while she worked on the book that, it was felt, might do very well—as, in fact, it did.

Peggy kicked off the fund-raising campaign with five hundred dollars and continued to support Emma while she worked on her memoir in a villa near Saint-Tropez. A young woman named Emily Coleman, a writer who had sent Goldman a fan letter in 1925, was hired to work as Emma's assistant and to edit her manuscript.

In her diary, Emily Coleman complained about Goldman's inability to write lucidly. "Sometimes it is more than I can bear." Coleman must have done a remarkable job of editing, because more than eighty years after its publication, *Living My Life* still seems not only clear but vivid and fully alive. The energy of Goldman's literary voice makes it easy to imagine how forceful she must have been. Much about her experience—addressing meetings, rallies, and labor strikes, traveling to meet fellow activists in Europe, working in factories and delivering babies, helping Berkman plot the Frick assassination and campaigning to free him from jail, taking lovers when she wished, even if she happened to be in love with two men at once—would have been news to Peggy, as would the seriousness with which Emma took her ideals, her work, her freedom to live however she wanted.

After some mutual hesitation, Peggy and Emily Coleman became friends. They shared a great deal in common. Both were American, living in Europe, and independently wealthy, though Coleman's monthly allowance was not so large as Peggy's inheritance. Both were obsessed with sex and would devote a good part of their lives to passionate and self-destructive love affairs. Emily believed that the only way to get to know someone was to have sex. Both women were mothers with erratic approaches to child-rearing—divorced from her husband, Emily had left her son John to be raised by a Russian governess outside Paris. Both had suffered nervous breakdowns: Peggy had experienced that little spell of picking up burned matches, but Emily's collapse had involved a stay in a mental institution where she was treated for a postpartum psychosis that became the subject of her first novel, *A Shutter of Snow* (1930).

Both women believed they were destined to live outside the bounds of conventional female domesticity and to invent new lives for themselves, though when they met, neither knew what sort of life that would be. Their close, if competitive and frequently tempestuous, friendship was to continue for decades, long outlasting either's connection with Emma Goldman, or with any of the men with whom they would become involved—the lovers whom on occasion they competed for or amicably passed along from one to the other.

Peggy's relationship with Emily Coleman was one of the female friendships that had a profound effect on her life—as it did on Coleman's. In their letters, they were uniquely open and honest with one another.

Emily Coleman's diaries provide the most intimate portrait of Peggy we have; they are far more revealing than *Out of This Century*, in which Peggy is more interested in amusing, entertaining, and shocking than in probing her own psyche or examining her choices. Throughout her journals, Emily records, more or less verbatim, her conversations with Peggy, and we hear Peggy's voice more clearly and (we assume) more accurately than we do in any other account of her life, including her own.

Frightened to leave her marriage, unable to imagine living on her own, hesitant to divorce a husband who beat and humiliated her, Peggy was buoyed by her new connection with Emma Goldman, who had once left a lover just because he didn't share her opinion of Nietzsche and who wrote, "Men had been able to do the world's work without the sustaining power of women; why should not also women? Or is it that woman needs love more than a man? A stupid, romantic notion, destined to keep her forever dependent on the male. Well, I would not have it; I would live and work without love. There is no permanency anywhere in nature or in life. I must drain the moment and then let the goblet fall to the ground."

In supporting Goldman, Peggy got a good return on her investment, as she so often did with the writers and artists she helped. It was useful for Peggy to have Emma nearby when she endured the shocks and dislocations of the late 1920s: the deaths of her sister and her two young nephews, and the end of her marriage.

Among the paradoxical aspects of Peggy Guggenheim's character was the division between her will and her desire to surrender that will to a man: to hand over every power except the power of her money. Given the conflict between her fear of independence and her fear of Laurence, she left her marriage in the only way she could: she fell in love with another man, one who was ready to leave his own life and take on the next phase of Peggy's education. In return she would manage—

and support—an elaborate bohemian household of interesting women more or less obsessed with the erotic magnetism of John Ferrar Holms.

Like Peggy, many people who knew John Holms agreed that he was a genius, but since he never produced much more than a few essays, a short story, and a poem or two, it may be that his genius was for making others regard him as a genius. In photos, he has the look of a tubercular, pre-Raphaelite satyr. He knew a great deal about poetry and had a number of strange party tricks, including the ability to run on all fours without bending his knees.

The poet Edwin Muir besottedly recalls Holms as "tall and lean, with a fine Elizabethan brow and auburn, curly hair, brown eyes with an animal sadness in them, a large, somewhat sensual mouth, and a little pointed beard which he twirled when he was searching for a word." According to Djuna Barnes, Holms seldom finished a sentence, but others, including Peggy, considered him a brilliant conversationalist.

In Gerhardie's *Mortal Love*, Holm appears as "Bonzo, so called by his friends for a reason they could no longer remember . . . He was a man of letters who in his early twenties had written a few promising trifles but had too long delayed taking the plunge, and there was accordingly an air of defensive disdain in his attitude to men and women who might ignore his worth. . . . [He] was only happy with artists and writers who looked on him as their equal and preferably as their superior." Though Gerhardie admired Holms, he also makes it clear that Holms's conversation contained more ellipses than full sentences, more suggestion than substance. Judging a fellow poet's poems, Bonzo opines, "They are uneven . . . but have something in them only to be found in poets of genuine worth, which, unless it is a mere freak, will inevitably lead . . . though, of course, it is foolish . . . to attempt to foretell . . . but there you are . . . they are poems."

Emily Coleman was in love with Holms, though their brief affair had come to nothing. And she too believed that he possessed a prodigious intellect. "He is the only person I have known who lives only in the fundamental chrysalis and not in the windings of the cocoon. He has a brain of steel, and he has built life from within his brain." Passages in Coleman's diary reproduce her conversations with John Holms, whom in early entries she calls Agamemnon. These talks made her feel as if she was the recipient of transcendent wisdom, but her readers are more likely to conclude that the dispenser of this transformative knowledge was manipulative and pretentious. "He said I am a genius, a child of genius, but I have known passion only as an adolescent knows it, which is not at all." Later in the diary, Coleman reports reading these pronouncements aloud to her friends, who decide, not unreasonably, that Holms sounds like "a dreadfully smug and conceited moralist."

According to a BBC writer named Lance Sieveking, in the BBC magazine *The Listener*, "Holms had a way of producing some obscure fifteenth-century poet . . . and, in broken sentences, extolling his genius to the detriment of all other reputations. His method of argument was a process of removing other people's examples with a melancholy chuckle, as hardly worthy of serious consideration, until only his obscure example remained in possession of the field, an easy victor, far, far ahead of all the others in perception, penetration, technique, profundity, and truth. There were a few of the more generally accepted names to which he would grant greatness. Among them were Donne, Blake, and Shakespeare, but even they had written much that was not worthy, a sad business."

If Holms was a bit of a charlatan, his magic worked on Peggy.

> When I first met him I was like a baby in kindergarten, but by degrees he taught me everything and sowed the seeds in

me that sprouted after he was no longer there to guide me.
. . . He held me in the palm of his hand and from the time
I once belonged to him to the day he died he directed my
every move, my every thought. . . . His chief desire was to
remold me, and he felt in me the possibilities that he was
later to achieve. . . . He saw the underlying meanings of everything. He knew why everybody wrote as they did, made
the kind of films they made or painted the kind of pictures
they painted. To be in his company was equivalent to living
in a sort of undreamed of fifth dimension. . . . He was the
only person I have ever met who could give me a satisfactory
reply to any question. He never said, "I don't know."

Many of the lessons that Peggy had learned from Goldman had apparently failed to take hold, and Holms—whom
Emma disliked—helped turn Peggy against her activist friend.
(The rift between Peggy and Emma widened after the publication of *Living My Life*, when Peggy felt she hadn't been given
sufficient credit for supporting its author.) In any case Peggy
readily allowed Holms to play Pygmalion to her naïve and un-
formed Galatea. Passion is distracting, and Peggy had many
things from which she wished to be distracted.

The night on which Holms and Peggy were introduced
by Emily Coleman was the first anniversary of Benita's death.
Added to the list of reasons for which Peggy had begun to despise Laurence Vail was her conviction that he had kept her
from seeing her sister; and now her sister was dead. Peggy's
grief and rage spiked when Laurence tore up some photos of
Benita that Peggy had placed around her room.

Despite the sad anniversary, Laurence (who shared with
Peggy and many of their friends a horror of being bored)
insisted that he and Peggy go out dancing. At a bistro in
Saint-Tropez, Peggy got drunk and wound up dancing on the
table.

This must have made an impression on John Holms, but all I remember now is that he took me to a tower and kissed me. That certainly made an impression on *me*, and I can attribute everything that followed to that simple little kiss.

Holms and Peggy were both married (a common-law marriage, in Holms's case) to other people, which added to the drama of their involvement. They met secretly, until Laurence Vail found out and threatened to kill Holms. It was all very thrilling, and in the end Peggy left Vail and took John Holms away from his sad, Irish amateur astrologer, an older woman named Dorothy.

Peggy's analysis of why John preferred her to Dorothy reveals less about her rival than about how she saw herself. "I think one reason John was so attracted to me was that I was just the opposite of Dorothy. I took life rather less seriously and never fussed. I joked about everything and he brought out my unconscious wit. . . . I was completely irresponsible and had so much vitality that I was sure I was quite a new experience for him. I was light and Dorothy was heavy."

After many delays and arguments, Peggy and Laurence agreed on the terms of their divorce. Peggy would retain legal guardianship of Pegeen and Laurence of Sindbad, who would visit Peggy for sixty days a year. Peggy found the separations from Sindbad difficult. Seeing him in Paris for the first time since the breakup "was a painful experience and released all the suppressed agony I felt over losing him." She mentions the journeys she made to pick up and return the children and describes the strong emotions she felt at each reunion and parting, along with her fury at Kay Boyle (whom Vail met soon after the separation and married in 1932) for trying to turn the children against her.

The divorce took a toll on Pegeen, who became so attached to her nanny Doris (the most stable and reliably loving presence in her life) that Doris's annual vacations were trau-matic. There were periods when Peggy, infatuated by Holms and struggling with Vail, more or less forgot Pegeen, who was left in Doris's care. Alone with her mother, Pegeen "clung to me like ivy to the oak and would not let me out of her sight. She was the most beautiful thing I have ever seen at this age. Her hair was platinum blond, and her skin was like fresh fruit. She was still under four years of age, and living under these uncertain conditions upset her considerably. When once I tried to leave her in Paris for a few days (with friends) she went on strike and I had to take her with me. She felt abandoned and frightened."

---◆◆◆---

Hayford Hall

AMONG THE things that Peggy most enjoyed was house-hunting, especially in the company of a man with whom she was in love. John Glassco had met her and Laurence Vail at one such moment in Provence, and had concluded that they were a happy couple.

Indeed, one of Peggy's great gifts was for finding beautiful and interesting places in which to live. Early on, houses were what she most willingly spent her money on, and what seemed to make her happiest. Later she would siphon part of those energies into collecting art. Her ultimate triumph was not only to amass a great art collection but to find a beautiful and interesting home, the Palazzo Venier dei Leoni, in which her art could continue to live—and to find that home on her own, knowing that she would probably not be living there with a man.

With John Holms, the search for a suitable dwelling lasted for years, because where to stay was only one of the questions

Holms was unable to decide. Finally they settled on Hayford Hall, a somewhat musty old mansion in a beautiful setting in Devon, where they lived in the summers of 1932 and 1933. The house was surrounded by gardens, a tennis court, and two lily ponds; an unspoiled natural wilderness began at the edge of their manicured lawns, and at night Peggy and her friends watched rabbits scurry across the grounds.

Like the Swiss villa shared by Byron and the Shelleys, or the Brooklyn Heights house where Auden, Capote, Paul and Jane Bowles, and Carson McCullers lived, or the country homes of William Morris's devotees, Hayford Hall was one of literary history's heady experiments in group living. At its center was John Holms, a writer who didn't write, surrounded by adoring women who did.

The best known of these writers was Djuna Barnes. During the summer of 1933, while her friends rode horses and went for rambles on the moor, Barnes stayed inside and composed much of her modernist novel *Nightwood*, in the rococo bedroom that, Peggy decided, was perfect for her; Barnes dedicated the novel to Peggy and John Holms. Another frequent visitor was the British author Antonia White, whose first novel, *Frost in May*, was published in 1933. The group archivist was Emily Coleman, who (aside from Peggy) was closest to John Holms and was consequently the object of the others' envy and resentment. In her diary, Emily recorded the conversations and conflicts that erupted when the group convened in the great hall for after-dinner high jinks involving intense sexual tension and rivalry, necking, insults, literary discussions, arguments, and (most often) long drunken monologues by Holms.

Peggy kept the household running and managed the servants, among them a French cook and the faithful Doris, who presided over the children's wing, where Pegeen lived, along with Sindbad Vail and Emily Coleman's son Johnny, when the boys came to visit. Peggy claimed to like spending time with the children, but in fact they were only rarely allowed in the main hall, and the other adults took only a moderate interest in them.

John Holms was kind to Pegeen, but the women were less friendly to Sindbad, who struck Emily as "too ordinary, like a comic strip boy." Coleman found Pegeen "more interesting. . . . She is a demon, and hard, but has such guts." Later, Sindbad's "ordinariness"—he much preferred sports to art—generated friction between him and Peggy, while Pegeen's "artistic" temperament would become, for her mother, a source of pride, concern, and ultimately grief.

Perhaps it was just as well that the children were shielded from the adults, whose gatherings involved much frank talk about sex, and whose after-dinner games of Truth, based on a game popular among the Parisian Surrealists, were essentially group inquisitions into the erotic fantasies and experiences of the other players.

All the women at Hayford Hall appear to have been in love with Holms. The fact that Peggy had invited a group of romantic rivals to share a house with her and her lover suggests that she may have chosen high drama over the more placid, potentially tepid satisfactions of domestic contentment. Or perhaps she was afraid that John Holms would otherwise get bored, since she considered herself his intellectual inferior.

Emily Coleman records conversations in which Peggy claimed to feel that she was beneath her friends "because they are artists and intellectuals and she isn't, and consequently look down on her." Peggy "said she could not tackle abstract ideas, that she was a little jealous when we talked intellectually." For Peggy, the consolation was that her connection with Holms was a passionately sexual one, and—at least according to Holms— "a man of talent does not want an intellectual woman, he wants to give way to his instinct."

Predictably, this agreement—that the sexually alluring

woman need not also have a brain—turned sour. Peggy informed Holms, "I admire your superiority complex, but you go too far." Coleman observed Holms telling Peggy "things that hurt her pride—he told her she knew nothing when she met him and he was trying to teach her something about life. He said she lived in other people's opinions and thought nothing of herself, that she lived in reactions, like all Americans." Later Emily would hear Holms calling Peggy a fool when she said "something stupid."

Though the savvy that Peggy showed in finding the right art advisers, in acquiring and preserving her collection, and in surrounding herself with interesting people suggests the presence of an acute intelligence, she nonetheless cultivated a partly natural, partly affected air of goofy abstraction—of missing the point, of understanding things only obliquely, a childlike naïveté that allowed her to say funny (and often quite mean and hurtful) things with the insouciance of a young girl. According to John Richardson, "She acted like someone's dumb younger sister, and it made you feel quite protective of her. She never grew up. She often seemed quite lost in the world, the way a sixteen- or seventeen-year-old girl might be lost."

At Hayford Hall, many evenings ended in a fierce argument because Peggy wanted John to come to bed and he preferred to stay up drinking and talking to the other women. Once when Peggy complained, John informed her that she "was pea-brained, and that his friends wondered why he lived with her." Coleman describes a bitter fight that began when she criticized Peggy for having interrupted John, and which culminated in Peggy ordering Emily to leave Hayford Hall—an order she soon rescinded.

In Gerhardie's novel, Peggy's alter ego, Molly, is described as "gloomily ironic," patiently waiting to go to bed while Bonzo (Holms) talks and talks." Hesitant to participate in the verbal pyrotechnics, "Molly, as always, said very little. Her face had a vague look. If she opened her mouth, it was to give vent to a general unfocused irony."

Though Djuna Barnes was predominantly a lesbian, she had had affairs with men, and a passage from Coleman's diary describes Barnes's flirtation with Holms during an evening that demonstrated just how murky the group's shifting loyalties and boundaries could become. Djuna, who had just washed her thick red hair, "began to get very loving with John." Waking up from a nap on the couch, Peggy noted, "This looks like rape." As Barnes continued to embrace Holms, Peggy predicted, "He'll assert his lump," and went on to make a remark that tied Holms's erection to the likelihood of her continued financial support. "If you rise, the dollar will fall." When John told Barnes that she had written the best work of any woman in fifty years, Djuna kissed his neck.

> Then she began to pound Peggy in the bottom, and Peggy shrieked, "My God, how this woman hates me," and Djuna kept pounding her, then began to pound me. She hadn't hit me four times before I had an orgasm.

Coleman also records a series of Peggy's witty remarks, several of which also appear in *Out of This Century*, where they provide the reader with a vivid if not especially appealing picture of Peggy's sense of humor. "Peggy is witty because she isn't trying, she has the gift, and does not think of any audience." During a discussion of whether women should wear makeup in the country, Peggy told Emily that she looked like the Ancient Mariner, "weatherbeaten." She informed Djuna Barnes that when Barnes read her work aloud, her face was like that of a baby wanting its bottle.

Increasingly, Peggy's barbed remarks were aimed at John Holms. When she tried to prevent Sindbad from carrying a pair of scissors, John asked why a ten-year-old couldn't carry a pair of scissors, and Peggy replied, "You're thirty-five and can't bring anything." One night she referred to John as "a wash-out."

By the end of the summer of 1932, Peggy said of John, "What do I care what his genius is, it does me no good. He doesn't use it." When Emily said that John gave her a sense of life, Peggy replied, "He gives me a sense of death." "He's told me a lot of things I want to know, but my he tries to pile on a lot that I *don't* want." John, was intelligent, Peggy agreed, but he had no talent.

John was hurt and angered by Peggy's insults, and Emily recorded a scene that seems all too reminiscent of Peggy's marriage to Laurence Vail:

> I shut my door, then heard screams from Peggy's room. I heard, "You dirty little bitch, you falsify everything. You lie and lie, like a serpent." He kept on talking, and she did not reply, after the screams died down. He said he could not stand her malice and venom.
>
> I knew she had probably accused him when he came up, and probably said it was later than it was, and he had hit her.

Obviously, we know better than to blame the victim of domestic abuse. But given that nearly all of Peggy's major romantic relationships contained some element of physical violence, we can only assume that either she had spectacular bad luck in her choice of men or that, for her, love may have involved a compulsion to bait her lovers into losing control. Emily Coleman describes an evening, at a Paris brasserie, early in Peggy's affair with John Holms. In full view of Holms, Peggy went to sit with Laurence Vail. Peggy and John had been quarreling, and "she did this to pique him. She is like a child playing with dynamite."

In the early winter of 1933, Peggy "got drunk one night and became very bitchy and taunted John about Garman." This was Douglas Garman, the handsome avant-garde publisher whom

John had been trying to persuade to publish Djuna Barnes's novel *Ryder.* When Peggy and Garman met at London's Chandos pub, they were instantly drawn to each other. Garman asked to come and stay with Peggy and John, who were then living in Paris.

> When he came I fell in love with him. . . . I imagine I felt Garman was a real man and John was more like Christ or a ghost. I needed someone human to make me feel like a woman again. John was indifferent to the worldly aspects of life and did not care how I looked or what I wore. Garman, on the contrary, noticed everything and commented on my clothes, which I found very pleasant.

When Peggy told Holms about her attraction to Garman, "John nearly killed me. He made me stand for ages naked in front of the open window [in December] and threw whiskey in my eyes. He said, 'I would like to beat your face so that no man will ever look at it again.' I was so frightened that I made Emily stay all night to protect me."

Much of what transpired during Peggy's life with John Holms, like much of what had occurred with Laurence Vail, was surely related to the massive amounts of alcohol being consumed. Hayford Hall became known, among Peggy's friends, as Hangover Hall.

Peggy complained about Holms's paralysis of will, his inability to do or decide anything, but no one seems to have related his passivity to the alcoholism from which he had suffered from an early age, and which was exacerbated by his term as a prisoner during World War I, in a camp where he and his fellow inmates (among them Alec Waugh) had nothing to do and unlimited access to cheap white wine. When Peggy refers to John's drinking, it's mostly in an oblique or offhand way, as a joke: she records an anecdote about some house guests who drank as much as John did and were sick for days. Alternately, her references to Holms's drinking are inflected with a flat, mocking affect. "When he drank a lot he always complained, saying, 'I'm so bored, so bored,' as though this cry came from his very depths and caused him great pain." Only later, in conversation with Emily Coleman, did Peggy say that even if John were somehow to return from the dead, she would never again be able to live with his drinking.

Edwin Muir's analysis of his friend's unhappiness also fails to mention alcohol: "The act of writing was itself an enormous obstacle to him, although his one ambition was to be a writer. His knowledge of his weakness, and his fear that in spite of his gifts, which he never doubted, he would not succeed in producing anything, intensified his stationary combat and reduced him to shaking impotence. He was persecuted by dreadful dreams and nightmares."

If alcohol ramped up the intensity and the erotic daring of Hayford Hall's summer residents, the tragedy that ended these romantic summer idylls was an indicator of how dangerous John Holms's inability to quit drinking, even for one evening, had become.

In August 1933, at the end of Peggy and John's second and final summer in Devon, John broke his wrist in a riding accident. The break was set badly by a local doctor, and John remained in pain, even after the couple returned to London in the autumn. A Harley Street doctor suggested a simple operation that required general anesthesia, but which could be performed at home.

The surgery was scheduled for January 18. The night before, John stayed up late, drinking with friends. The next morning his hangover was so severe that Peggy considered canceling the operation, but, having once postponed the procedure because John had the flu, she was embarrassed to do so again.

After a long time had elapsed since the start of the surgery, Peggy became alarmed. Soon after, the doctors informed her that John was dead. The anesthetic had caused his heart to fail. Later, an autopsy report revealed that "all of John's organs were very much affected by alcohol and he was in rather bad shape. The doctors were exonerated."

Peggy records her complicated—and telling—response to John's death. At first she was certain that she would never be happy again, a conviction that alternated with relief. "It was as though I were suddenly released from a prison. I had been John's slave for years and I imagined for a moment I wanted to be free, but I didn't at all. I did not have the slightest idea how to live or what to do. . . . After John died I was in perpetual terror of losing my soul. . . . I believe that in the future life some day I will find John again and my soul will be safe."

But Peggy did not—and at that point in her life *could* not—remain alone for long. A solution occurred to her when she received a condolence letter from Douglas Garman. "I began to think about [Garman] again, and by degrees I realized that I would use him to save me from my misery."

Separated from his wife and the father of a daughter named Debbie, who was Pegeen's age, Douglas Garman seemed at first to be precisely the savior Peggy needed. Their affair, which began eight weeks after John Holms's death, was initially very romantic; Garman wrote a poem about their love that included the unfortunate phrase "the gift between your thighs." But Peggy felt guilty for having taken a new lover so soon and for having momentarily wished that John Holms was dead.

Peggy's guilt prolonged the grief that kept returning to spoil whatever moments of contentment she and Garman might otherwise have shared. She couldn't stop comparing Garman with John or from telling the living lover how much she missed the dead one, even as Garman continued to hope that she would recover so they could have a peaceful life.

In fact their chances of leading such a life were slim at best.

As soon as their passion cooled even slightly, Peggy grew disenchanted with the lonely, uneventful country existence she was leading with Garman, Pegeen, Debbie, and Garman's mother, who lived nearby. She missed Holms and the wild nights at Hayford Hall; she longed for those abusive games of Truth, those drunken fits of hysterics. Holms had been a genius, a great artist, while Garman was a boring Communist who surrounded himself with party functionaries and strangers he admired merely for being working class.

When he and Peggy met, Garman, the son of a wealthy doctor, was working for his brother-in-law, a publisher named Ernest Wishart. Like Holms, Garman wanted to be a writer, but he also found it nearly impossible to write. He had been to Russia and thought of himself as a revolutionary, though Peggy was quick to point out that he remained a creature of his class, driving her Hispano-Suiza to deliver lectures on the inevitability of a workers' revolution. Garman's nephew Michael Wishart describes his difficulty, as a boy, reconciling the art ("a crucified kipper") that hung in Peggy and Garman's bedroom with his uncle's politics, "but I enjoyed the Marxist heated swimming pool, of course."

Influenced by Lucille Kohn and Emma Goldman, Peggy had long sympathized with left-wing causes; Laurence Vail had mocked her willingness to support unions and striking workers. But Peggy was irked by what she saw as Garman's hypocrisy, his unshakeable regard for Stalin, and his increasingly puritanical disapproval of art, literature—and nearly everything she cared about. Eventually Peggy became a member of the Communist Party, though in her memoirs she explains it as a sort of experiment she conducted to prove that Garman was wrong when he'd insisted that she'd have to agree to work for the party in order to join.

At first she and Garman concealed their affair, because it had begun so soon after Holms died and because she hoped to shield her children from the knowledge that Holms—to whom Pegeen had become deeply attached—had been supplanted by a new lover. Such instances of tact and delicacy were rare on Peggy's part, who more often failed to distinguish her own needs, emotions, and desires from her son and daughter's. Not only was Pegeen mourning Holms, but she was also grief-stricken by the loss of Doris. Pegeen's nanny had briefly left the household to get married, but when Doris offered to return to work after her wedding, Peggy was so jealous of her daughter's affection for the baby nurse that she refused to take her back.

That Easter, Peggy traveled to Austria to spend the holiday with both children and with Laurence Vail, who—unlike Garman—was endlessly willing to comfort Peggy and listen to her talk about how much she missed John Holms. When she returned to England, Garman drove her to Sussex, where he had bought a house for his mother near the picturesque but "absolutely dead" village of South Harting. That summer, Peggy rented Warblington Castle, near Garman's mother, and invited Debbie Garman to stay with her and Pegeen.

Peggy's friends, including Emily Coleman and Antonia White, came for long visits, but the women desperately missed John Holms and were disinclined to accept Garman as his replacement. Emily considered him a fool and began to refer to him, in her diaries, as Garbage. Djuna Barnes said that Garman "wasn't human, he was 'a doll that says Communism when you pinch its stomach.'"

After a trip to Wales, Peggy decided to rent a house near Mrs. Garman so that Pegeen could attend school in the country with Debbie. When no suitable home could be found to lease, Garman persuaded Peggy to buy Yew Tree Cottage, in the town of Petersfield. The house, which dated from the Elizabethan era, was charming, the setting beautiful, but Peggy was miserable.

Soon after I took this step I decided to commit suicide, I was still so unhappy about John. I therefore put the house in Garman's name as I intended to die. Of course I didn't and I went to live in the house instead.

Peggy threw herself into country life, supervising a gardener and "a darling little Italian maid," and—insofar as she was capable of it—devoting herself to Pegeen. Just after Christmas, Garman and Debbie moved in. Peggy notes with satisfaction that two girls grew very close, and that the mature, intellectual, well-behaved Debbie exerted a positive influence on Pegeen.

Peggy wrote to Emily Coleman to say that she enjoyed being alone when Garman was in London and that, given enough peace and quiet, she felt that she might be able to write something. She was reading a great deal, from Henry Miller to Tolstoy, from William Blake to Céline. She also wrote a review of Emily's novel *Tygon*, and kept a diary, much of it about John. But something—perhaps guilt over writing about one man while she was living with another—inspired her to burn the diary in the autumn of 1935.

By then she had begun to lose patience with Garman— whom she persuaded to give up his publishing job and try to write in the studio he built at the end of the garden—and with the longueurs of her bucolic life. The description of Garman's character that appears in *Out of This Century* contains intimations of what would soon go wrong. The paragraph begins with praise. "Garman was a straightforward, honest person with a wonderful sense of humor, and a fine mimic," and ends on a note of complaint. "He was five years younger than I which made me self-conscious. He found me very sloppy and would have liked me to dress much better than I did. He did not like me to have any gray hair."

Over time, Peggy felt increasingly isolated. It seemed to her that she was always nursing Pegeen and Debbie, who were perpetually coming down with colds and the flu, because the house was drafty and cold; she describes herself lying in bed, reading, wearing fur gloves and shivering. As the tension between Peggy and Garman escalated, his puritanical strain emerged. He disapproved of Peggy's reading her beloved Proust and insisted that she should be reading Karl Marx instead.

According to Emily Coleman, Peggy and Garman were not in the least congenial; they had no common interests, didn't like the same people or the same things. The situation between them was growing more obviously painful. Garman disapproved of Peggy's drinking, but, she writes, "for some perverse reason I now found it necessary to do so," though, she recalls somewhat unconvincingly, she had "indulged very seldom" when she'd lived with Vail and Holms. Peggy not only continued to compare Garman unfavorably with Holms, but she informed Garman that he'd bored Holms and that the only reason Holms had come to see him in London was because he had hoped that Garman might publish Djuna's novel.

By the time Peggy and Garman had lived together for a year and a half, she had decided to run away from him and did, though she kept coming back. Meanwhile, yet another love affair turned violent. "He still loved me very much, though I did everything to destroy it. . . . Once I was so awful to him that he slapped me hard in the face and then was so ashamed of himself that he burst into tears."

Peggy found solace in longs walks and in reading. Garman officially joined the Communist Party and funded party causes with Peggy's money. When Garman began giving lectures suggesting that all great writers were revolutionary, Peggy attended and "asked questions to embarrass and confuse him. After John's brilliant mind and detachment, all this was too silly for me to endure." Annoyed by Garman's piety and faux-asceticism, "I became like a bull when it sees red. Only in my case I saw red every time I heard Communism mentioned."

In the summer of 1936, Peggy traveled to Venice, where

she enjoyed being alone, going wherever she pleased, eating when she wanted to, and studying the Carpaccios in the museum. But after her return, the discord at home worsened. One summer night, Garman hit Peggy again and again, and she reported to Emily that she experienced a great relief; the violence had thawed the frozen state in which they had been living.

Peggy had made a bet with Garman: if Edward VIII gave up the throne in order to marry Wallis Simpson, Garman would have to marry her. But after the Duke of Windsor's abdication, Garman refused to honor the bet. In fact, he insisted, their love was over; Peggy had killed his affection for her. The couple decided to separate, and Garman moved to London, though they continued to vacation together. He visited on weekends—and insisted on sleeping with Peggy.

One weekend, "Garman and I had a row about Communism. And I got so bitchy that he hit me. I slipped and fell. There was blood everywhere." Though the couple spent most of their time apart, the affair dragged on for another unhappy few months.

In the summer of 1937, Peggy's mother, critically ill with lung cancer, visited Europe. In Paris, she took a suite at the Hotel Crillon, where Peggy and the children joined her. Together Peggy and Florette toured the International Exhibition in Paris, and though her mother was the one who was dying, Peggy told Emily Coleman that she felt that her own life was over, to which her friend replied unhelpfully, "If you feel that way, perhaps it is."

1
Peggy Guggenheim in a dress by Paul Poiret, 1925

2

Laurence Vail as a young man

3

From left, John Holms, Djuna Barnes, Antonia White,
and Peggy Guggenheim at Hayford Hall, ca. 1932–33

4

Peggy Guggenheim on the terrace of her apartment,
Île Saint-Louis, Paris, ca. 1940

5
Group photograph of "Artists in Exile," New York, 1942

6

Surrealist Gallery, Art of this Century, 28–30 West 57th Street, New York, 1942.
Frederick Kiesler, architect

7

Peggy Guggenheim and Jackson Pollock in front of Pollock's *Mural* (1943) in
the first-floor entrance hall of Guggenheim's residence, 155 East 61st Street,
New York, ca. 1946. Partially visible in the foreground is an unidentified
David Hare sculpture.

8
Portrait of Pegeen Vail Guggenheim

9
Peggy Guggenheim in her living room, Venice, 1968

10 *(facing page)*
Peggy Guggenheim

11
Exterior of the Peggy Guggenheim Collection, Venice

Guggenheim Jeune

NINETEEN THIRTY-SEVEN was a watershed year for Peggy. She was about to turn forty. Her separation from Garman marked the first time that she had left a man without having another man waiting in the wings. Her sudden and mostly frightening independence made her aware that for fifteen years she had never been "anything but a wife." In fact, she had never been anything but a wife, a daughter, a friend, a mother, and a rich woman who could surround herself with entertaining friends. Only after her life with Garman ended did Peggy first begin to appreciate the advantages and pleasures of independence, of serious work, and to admit the possibility that she possessed an "inner self" with its own integrity, demands, and satisfactions.

Though her letters and her memoir make it clear that she had more literary talent than Laurence Vail, John Holms, or Douglas Garman, Peggy assumed, and had been encouraged to believe, that she had no gift for making art, for painting or writing. But during the protracted and unpleasant conclusion of her affair with Garman, Peggy began to wonder whether there was some profession she could go into, one that would let her make use of her natural gifts, her money and her connections.

Peggy thanks her close friend Peggy Waldman for being the first to propose that she either start a publishing house or open an art gallery in London. But the wording of the letter that Waldman sent in May 1937—"I wish you'd do some serious work—the art gallery, book agency—anything that would be engrossing yet impersonal"—implies that the idea is not a new one; *the* art gallery suggests that the two women may have discussed this possibility before. And in a letter to Emily Coleman, written later that spring, Peggy Guggenheim mentions Garman's attempt to talk her out of this new venture. Peggy claims that she rejected the idea of a publishing house because it promised to be too expensive. Presumably, the gallery sounded as if it would be cheaper and more fun. "Little did I dream of the thousands of dollars I was about to sink into art."

Peggy soon began to take the idea seriously. Opening a gallery would allow her to spend time with artists, to resume a way of life she'd come to value more than ever during those lonely months in the country with Garman and the children. It would enable her to do something useful and productive with her money and to continue supporting people whose talent she believed in—something she'd already been doing, in a casual way, for decades.

Assisted by his mistress, the baroness Hilla Rebay, Peggy's Uncle Solomon had begun amassing a large collection of modern art, and the prospect of competing with, and perhaps surpassing, the baroness strongly appealed to Peggy. Better yet, Peggy's newfound vocation would unnerve her family and their stodgy friends. A daughter of the Guggenheims would be running her own business, living independently, buying and selling art. She would be showing the work of the Surrealists, which—with its emphasis on the irrational, on the unconscious, and on sex—was shocking in itself. Certainly it was no accident Peggy's first show in her London gallery featured drawings that Jean Cocteau had done on bedsheets, and which included his lover's pubic hair covered over with leaves.

As Peggy searched for an adviser who would introduce her to the right people, she began an affair with a young painter named Humphrey Jennings. Talented and well connected, Jennings was—along with Herbert Read, André Breton, and the British painter Roland Penrose—one of the organizers of an important 1936 show of Surrealist art in London. Somewhat uncharacteristically, Douglas Garman had suggested that Peggy attend this "First Surrealist Exhibition," but Peggy—convinced that Surrealism was no longer of any interest—had elected to ignore it.

In *Out of This Century*, Peggy explains that Emily Coleman had had an affair with Jennings but had grown tired of him—and passed him along to Peggy. Emily's version is quite different. In love with Jennings, Emily begged Peggy (who had admitted to being sexually attracted to Jennings) to leave him alone. But Emily knew she was no match for Peggy—and what Peggy could offer. "What I mean to him as a person scarcely exists. He wants an American who will be passionately worshipping him, understanding him, giving him violent sexual satisfaction: docile. Peggy. Also the money. What does money mean to him—a lot." This may be the only time in Peggy Guggenheim's life (and certainly in Coleman's diary) that Peggy was referred to as docile. But Emily was right about Peggy's appeal; Coleman was no match for her friend's sexuality—or for her money. Peggy went off with Jennings, leaving Emily in what she described as a suicidal state.

When Peggy went to stay with her mother in Paris in the summer of 1937, Jennings had come over from England to join her. He brought Peggy to meet André Breton, and she in turn introduced Jennings to Marcel Duchamp. Together Peggy and Humphrey went to see Yves Tanguy, and Jennings outlined some (according to Peggy) wild and incomprehensible proposals for how they might show Tanguy's art—ideas about exhibition design that may well have influenced the plans for Art of This Century.

The shared dream of running a gallery was initially exciting, but Peggy wasn't physically attracted to Jennings, with his "ugly emaciated body" and "Donald Duck" looks. And her inability to fall in love with him seems to have poisoned their professional partnership; Peggy reported feeling happy when she got rid of Jennings. Planning and operating the gallery would be more fun without him.

Jennings wept when he realized that he would have to abandon his fantasy of a "wonderful life with me, surrounded by luxury, gaiety, and Surrealism." But once this awkwardness had passed, Peggy and Humphrey Jennings became good friends and went off to the 1937 Paris Exposition, which Peggy had visited with Florette. "There for the first time I was able to study modern art."

Peggy neglects to describe what she saw there, so eager is she to note the fact that Douglas Garman came to Paris and was surprised when she rented one hotel room for them both. Throughout this period, she was still vacillating about whether or not to remain with Garman, despite how unhappy they'd made each other. Garman enjoyed Paris, where he was delighted that the leftist Popular Front was in power. But he sagely rejected Peggy's suggestion that they get back together.

Garman spent time with Peggy at the exposition, where the massive Palace of the Soviets was crowned with a statue of two Russian workers brandishing a hammer and sickle. The Soviet pavilion directly faced the equally aggressive German pavilion; together they flanked the Eiffel Tower. Designed by

Albert Speer, the German pavilion had, at its summit, a swastika and the National Socialist eagle.

There was a great deal of modern art for Peggy to study at the Exposition Internationale des Arts et Techniques dans la Vie Moderne. Focused on the gallery that she planned to open, she looked at art more seriously and with a different eye than she had in the past. The showpiece of the exposition was Picasso's *Guernica*, which the artist had painted several months after having been invited by the Spanish government to contribute a large work to the Spanish Pavilion and only a few days after hearing about the German bombing of the Basque town. At the same pavilion was a mural by Joan Miró and a fountain sculpted by Alexander Calder; on exhibit in the other buildings were works by Léger and Delaunay, and, in the Pavilion of Electricity and Light, a huge painted panel, *The Electric Fairy*, by Dufy. At the Petit Palais, the curators of the Museum of Modern Art of the City of Paris showed works by Braque, Picasso, Matisse, and Maillol.

Peggy, who received $450,000 after the death of her mother in November 1937, hired a capable and energetic woman named Wyn Henderson, who had known John Holms, to manage her new gallery. It was Henderson who proposed that the gallery be called Guggenheim Jeune—to capitalize on Peggy's name (and on that of her Uncle Solomon) while at the same time suggesting that this venture would be younger, fresher, and more adventurous than her uncle's collection. Wyn found a space to rent at 30 Cork Street, and Peggy and Wyn decided to open the gallery as soon as possible after the lease took effect in January 1938.

A typographer by profession, Henderson designed the letterhead for Guggenheim Jeune, as well as the catalogues and invitations. Peggy credited her with having made "everything go like clockwork." Possessed of great tact and warmth, Wyn remembered the clients Peggy often failed to recognize. She was also a kindred spirit. Asked by Peggy to total her lovers, Wyn lost count at a hundred. "She was always egging me on to enjoy myself," Peggy writes.

While Wyn set up the gallery, Peggy began to look for artists to show. Through Mary Reynolds, she had met Marcel Duchamp, who would become the first and arguably the most influential of Peggy's advisers. Peggy's accounting of her debt to Duchamp is an expression not only of gratitude but also of the lingering "inferiority complex" reinforced by the condescension of so many people around her.

> At that time I couldn't distinguish one thing in art from another. Marcel tried to educate me. To begin with, he taught me the difference between Abstract and Surrealist art. Then he introduced me to all the artists. They all adored him, and I was well received wherever I went. He planned shows for me and gave me lots of advice. I have him to thank for my introduction to the modern art world.

Initially Peggy hoped to exhibit Brancusi's work, but the Romanian sculptor had temporarily left Paris, and Peggy approached Jean Cocteau, whose outrageous bedsheet drawings were sure to attract publicity for her inaugural show. The first viewers to be scandalized by Cocteau's nudes were the British customs officials, whom Peggy mollified, with Duchamp's help, by agreeing to show the Cocteau bedsheets only in her private office. Duchamp also introduced her to other artists, among them Kandinsky, Tanguy, and Jean Arp, whose 1933 bronze *Shell and Head* was, Peggy wrote, "the first thing I bought for my collection. . . . [Arp] took me to the foundry where it had been cast and I fell so in love with it that I asked to have it in my hands. The instant I felt it I wanted to own it." Such passages underline the fact that, for Peggy, owning art was a passion rather than a savvy business decision.

During this time, she wrote to Emily Coleman: "I am in

Paris working hard for my gallery and fucking." One can see, in this letter and in a subsequent one she sent Emily at the end of March, her old desire to shock combined with a new refusal to avoid the pattern that had caused her so much grief in the past: falling in love and letting herself be drawn into degrading and violent relationships. Even among Peggy's bohemian friends, the freedom she felt to have sex without any emotional involvement was unusual for a woman, and certainly rare for one who had come from the repressed society in which Peggy had been raised.

Reprimanded by Emily, who suggested that Peggy's erotic life was as self-destructive and worrisome as Djuna Barnes's drinking, Peggy replied:

> When you compare my fucking with Djuna's drinking I think you are wrong again. Djuna's whole life has collapsed because of her drinking. But my fucking is only a sideshow. My work comes first every time & my children are still there. Both the center of my life. Everyone needs sex & a man. It keeps one alive & loving & feminine. If you can't manage to make a life permanently with inferior people, & thank God I can't, you must still now & then indulge in a physical life and its consequence. . . . I find men & man really stimulating but now, thank God, I have my own strengths & my inner self to fall back on. John sowed the seeds for this & Garman made them grow by watering. The necessity of falling back on myself.

The letter is startling, not so much because of Peggy's unembarrassed acceptance of her own sexuality but because of the speed with which she has ceased playing the role of country mistress and housewife, patiently waiting for Garman to make one of his weekend appearances at their home, and become a woman who views Garman as one of the "inferior people" she can't make a life with—a woman who puts her work first and believes that she possesses an inner self to fall back on. Peggy's victory over her dependence on men was hardly a permanent one—later she would enter into relationships that were no less exploitative than the affairs of her youth—but still, she had undergone a remarkable change: she had tapped into the energy that would enable her to do the work for which she would be remembered.

But as we know, the surest way to fall in love is to forswear it. Even as Peggy was celebrating her new independence, she had become infatuated with a man who was fully as difficult as any of her previous lovers—but considerably more gifted. After years of trying to convince herself that her beloved was a genius, she had at last met an authentic one.

On the day after Christmas, 1937, Peggy attended a party at the home of Helen Joyce (who, when she was married to Leon Fleischman and having an affair with Laurence Vail, had helped persuade Peggy to move to Paris) and Helen's current husband, Giorgio Joyce, James Joyce's son. Among the guests was a young Irish writer named Samuel Beckett.

Though Peggy Guggenheim has been accused of chasing after famous men, it must be remembered that, at the time of their affair, Beckett was relatively unknown. He had published a small book on Proust, a short story collection, *More Pricks than Kicks*, and an essay on the "work in progress" that would become James Joyce's *Finnegans Wake*. Though Beckett had already achieved more than John Holms and Douglas Garman, Peggy had no way of knowing that he would go on to write one masterpiece after another, that he would win the Nobel Prize, or that his novels, plays, and stories would become canonical works of world literature. In the first edition of her memoir and in the stories she told her friends, Peggy's name for Beckett was Oblomov, after the hero of the eponymous Russian novel: a man who cannot gather the strength of will or the decisiveness required simply to get out of bed.

Beckett was very handsome, thin and slightly vulpine, with

prominent cheekbones and strikingly bright eyes. He was literary, eloquent: exactly Peggy's type. He was also ten years younger than she was. "A tall, lanky Irishman of about thirty with enormous green eyes that never looked at you. He wore spectacles, and always seemed to be far away solving some intellectual problem; he spoke very seldom and never said anything stupid. He was excessively polite, but rather awkward."

He walked Peggy home from the dinner at Helen and Giorgio's and asked to come upstairs, then awkwardly invited her to lie beside him on the sofa. They went to bed and stayed there until the next evening. "We might be there still," Peggy wrote, had she not agreed to have dinner with Jean Arp. Beckett left abruptly, saying, "Thank you, it was nice while it lasted."

Several days later they met again, on the street, by accident, though Peggy believed that it was not accidental, that she must have been looking for him without knowing it. Together they went to Mary Reynolds's apartment, where they stayed in bed, by Peggy's count, twelve days, though others—among them, Beckett's biographers—have claimed that this was an exaggeration.

In a letter to his friend, the poet Thomas McGreevy, Beckett wrote on January 5, 1938, "Peggy Guggenheim has been here and I have seen quite a lot of her. She is starting a gallery on Cork Street, opens on 22nd inst. with Cocteau drawings and furniture. Then there will be Kandinsky, Arp, Brancusi, Benno, etc. . . . I gave Guggenheim your address and she is anxious to get in touch with you at earliest op. She returns to London probably tomorrow. I hope something may come out of it for you."

The introverted Irish writer and the voluble American heiress might have seemed an unlikely couple, but both had a dry, ironic sense of humor and both cared deeply about art. Beckett not only talked Peggy out of her preference for the Old Masters by persuading her that modern art was "a living thing," but talked her into buying modern art, which he said was her duty. Peggy had always been a great reader and was eager to discuss literature—she and Beckett compared the relative merits of Céline and Joyce—in a way she hadn't been able to with Garman. Douglas Garman had tried to stop her from reading Proust—and Sam Beckett had written a book about him.

In addition, Beckett's erratic behavior made him irresistible to Peggy. He drank a great deal and was often drunk. Never knowing what he would do, or when he would appear, Peggy found herself falling in love. Quoted in Deirdre Bair's biography, a friend of Beckett's said, "She was sensual, taking—always interested in literature, but only in terms of what she could take from it or how it could be turned toward her. She recognized something in Sam, and I think she wanted to be a part of whatever good things were going to happen to him."

After decades of supporting a man's work, or the work that that man wasn't actually doing, this time Peggy was the one who had work to do, though Sam Beckett would have preferred her to stay in bed and drink. Preparations for the Cocteau show occupied most of her time, and Peggy remarked on the irony of having created a career for herself because she had no personal life only to have her personal life undone by her career.

Just before Peggy left for London, Beckett was stabbed in the chest when a stranger, asking for money, attacked him on the street. The wound was serious, and he was hospitalized and nursed by Suzanne Deschevaux-Dumesnil, a musician with whom he would live for years and whom he eventually married. Suzanne, wrote Peggy, "made curtains while I made scenes."

Beckett's affair with Peggy lasted, on and off, for thirteen months. But they would never again be as happy as they were, during those twelve—or however many—days they spent in bed at Mary Reynolds's apartment. In a 1973 interview, Peggy told Deirdre Bair, "I don't think he was in love with me for more than ten minutes. He couldn't make up his mind about anything. He wanted me around but he didn't want to have to do anything about it."

While preparing for the Cocteau show, Peggy attended the International Exposition of Surrealism, which opened on January 16, 1938, at the Galerie des Beaux-Arts. In the courtyard of the Galerie was Salvador Dalí's *Rainy Taxi*, a black hansom cab in which a female mannequin, covered with live snails, sprawled amid the junglelike vegetation that clogged the rain-soaked windows. Lining the entrance to the exposition were fifteen mannequins decorated by the artists to represent the objects of their desire; the head of André Masson's mannequin was encased in a birdcage housing a school of celluloid goldfish. The ceiling of the main room had been lined by Duchamp with twelve hundred coal sacks, while the floor was covered with dead leaves, banked toward the center, where a brazier glowed. The smell of roasting coffee filled the air, as did the sound of maniacal laughter, which had been recorded at a mental asylum. At the opening, the guests were given flashlights to help them make their way through the darkened rooms, which featured works by Giacometti, Ernst, Man Ray, Breton, Magritte, and Miró, as well as Meret Oppenheim's *Fur-Covered Cup*.

By now we have experienced decades of art installation: from the memory palaces of Ilya Kabokov to the riotous streetscapes of Red Grooms to the pilgrimage site that Marina Abramowicz created in the atrium of the Museum of Modern Art. But for the people who visited the Surrealist Exposition of 1938, the alternate world they entered was something entirely new.

One can easily understand why Peggy was so attracted to Surrealism. In her diary, Emily Coleman refers to Peggy's Surrealist sense of humor. Many of the tenets on which the movement was based—the desire to shock, to challenge and overturn convention, to unleash the unconscious, to engage in frank discussions of sex—seem like a description of Peggy's personality. For Peggy, visiting the exposition was a sudden immersion in an environment in which the secret and hidden was celebrated as art. Tentatively and gradually in Guggenheim Jeune, and later more overtly at Art of This Century, she re-created something akin to the museumgoing experience that the Surrealists had created in Paris.

Meanwhile, Duchamp was supervising the hanging of Cocteau's work at Peggy's gallery. Peggy left Paris for London, where Guggenheim Jeune opened on January 24, 1938.

The decision to begin with a show of Cocteau had been a wise one; his name was known in Great Britain, though mostly because of his writings and his film *The Blood of a Poet*. His visual art was less familiar to the British public and was well received by the press; reporters also noted the glamour of the opening, to which Peggy wore earrings made from brass curtain rings linked together.

Guggenheim Jeune's second show, a Kandinsky retrospective and the first show of his work in England, was even more successful than the Cocteau. Kandinsky and his "horrid" wife, wrote Peggy, arranged the exhibition, which featured paintings done from 1910 to 1937.

Solomon Guggenheim had been collecting Kandinksy's paintings but had been urged to stop because the Baroness Rebay had a lover, Rudolf Bauer, who considered Kandinsky a rival. When Peggy wrote to her uncle, suggesting that he buy a Kandinsky from her, she received a nasty letter from Baroness Rebay, informing Peggy that, should she and Solomon Guggenheim ever decide to buy a painting from a gallery instead of directly from the artist, Guggenheim Jeune would be the last place they would patronize. The baroness accused Peggy of exploiting the Guggenheim name, which had come to stand for "an ideal in art." Peggy, the baroness charged, was using the family name to sell paintings, "as if this great philanthropic work was intended to be a useful boost to some small shop."

The baroness also suggested—as it would turn out, with a certain sagacity and prescience—that Peggy start a collection instead of a commercial gallery: "This way you can get into useful contact with artists, and you can leave a fine collection to your country if you know how to choose." Peggy wrote back that she was amused by the baroness's letter, which Herbert Read had advised her to frame and hang on the wall of Guggenheim Jeune. And Peggy sent a copy of her reply to Uncle Solomon, together with a disclaimer: her intention was to help artists, not to profit from their work.

Peggy's response was more prophetic than she could have known or might have wished. Guggenheim Jeune was not commercially successful, but it did help to create and solidify the reputations of many artists who had been better known on the Continent than in England.

The Kandinsky show, from mid-February to mid-March, was praised by the British press in ways that made it clear that Guggenheim Jeune was not merely interested in creating a sensation, or in hosting chic gallery openings. The gallery was *serious*; it showed and sold important art. During the show, an art teacher from a public school in the north of England asked Peggy if he could show ten Kandinskys to his students. "Delighted" by the idea, and by the possibility of spreading the word about modern art, Peggy asked the artist, who agreed, provided that his work was insured. When the show closed, the teacher strapped the canvases to his car and drove them to his school; on returning the paintings, he reported that they had meant a great deal to the school.

Peggy continued traveling to Paris, where she visited artists, and where her romance with Beckett started and stopped. Together they attended a birthday party for James Joyce. Beckett gave his mentor a blackthorn walking stick, and Peggy helped him procure a type of Swiss wine that Joyce especially liked. Beckett claimed not to know whether he wanted to continue his affair with Peggy—or whether he wanted to sleep with her at all. Getting drunk together and walking around Paris all night became a substitute for sex.

Peggy claimed that her passion was inspired by her belief that Beckett "was capable of great intensity, and that I could bring it out. He, on the other hand, always denied it, saying he was dead and had no feelings that were human." And as had happened with other men, frustration and rejection fueled Peggy's ardor. One night, "I went home with him thinking how much less I should really like him if I ever had him. In fact, as he took my arm, I had the illusion of everything being settled and I thought, 'How boring.'" Peggy's ennui was short-lived. Once they reached Beckett's apartment, the terrified writer rushed off and left her alone.

Happily, Peggy was less easily wounded and buffeted by romantic upheaval than she had been in the past. In a letter to Emily Coleman, she again assured her friend that work was the center of her life, and that she was proud of how much she had already accomplished.

The next show at Peggy's gallery, of portraits by a relatively conventional British painter named Cedric Morris, was a less obvious choice. But a fracas at the exhibition—one of the portrait subjects attempted to burn the show's catalogues at the gallery, and Morris attacked him—generated useful publicity.

The Morris exhibition was followed by a group show of sculptures by artists including Arp, Brancusi, Henry Moore, and Alexander Calder. Once more the British customs agents interfered, invoking a law designed to protect the fabricators of grave markers by taxing imported stone. J. B. Manson, the director of the Tate Gallery, was called in to rule on whether the sculptures were art; if not, they would be subject to a costly import duty. Manson ruled that the sculptures were not art.

Wyn Henderson drew up a petition that was signed by art critics, among them Herbert Read and Clive Bell, protesting Manson's verdict. The case was brought to the House of Commons, and Guggenheim Jeune won. "Mr. Manson not only lost his case, but pretty soon his job as well. I thus rendered a great service to foreign artists and to England."

Though Peggy had given up hope for a future with Beckett, she agreed to show the work of Geer van Velde, a Dutch artist who was Beckett's friend and whose paintings he admired; the brief catalogue essay, which Beckett wrote, contained a highly compressed chronology of the painter's career ("Born the third of four April 5th 1898 at Lisse near Leyden. Tulips and Rembrandt") and the following lines, in which one can hear Beckett's literary voice: "Believes painting should mind its own business, *i.e.* colour. *i.e.* no more say Picasso than Fabritius, Vermeer. Or inversely."

Despite Beckett's suggestion that his friend's paintings owed as much to Vermeer as they did to Picasso, the British critics thought they resembled imitation Picassos. But because she loved Beckett, Peggy—cloaking her identity under different names—bought several of van Velde's canvases.

After the show closed, Peggy invited van Velde and his wife to spend a weekend at Yew Tree Cottage, where Beckett joined them. There Beckett confessed to Peggy that his affair with Suzanne had grown more serious. Peggy claimed not to mind; Suzanne, she believed, was unattractive and more of a mother than a lover. But on the chance that Beckett was capable of jealousy, Peggy had a short but public affair with the art dealer E. L. T. Mesens, who managed a gallery next door to her own and who edited a Surrealist journal, *The London Bulletin*, which produced Peggy's catalogues for free in return for a paid advertisement Peggy took in its pages. Peggy would have liked to share control of the paper, but Mesens was loyal to his coeditor, Humphrey Jennings.

Soon after, Beckett and Peggy, together with the van Veldes, drove to the south of France. On the way back, Beckett booked a room with twin beds and refused to share Peggy's. In the morning, they walked all over Dijon, visiting museums. Peggy told Beckett how much nicer he had become; Beckett was relieved that Peggy no longer made scenes. Their time together was so amicable that they "parted with sorrow, Beckett as usual regretting he relinquished me."

In early July, Guggenheim Jeune showed the Surrealist moonscapes of Yves Tanguy, whom Peggy had met in Paris and with whom she was very much taken. She found Tanguy and his wife, who had never before visited England, to be "unspoiled and so different from all the blasé people that I knew that it was a pleasure to be with them." Peggy was delighted with the way the Tanguy show looked, and, in her memoir, describes it with more enthusiasm than any other exhibition at Guggenheim Jeune.

Peggy bought a Tanguy painting entitled *Le Soleil dans son écrin*, which, she writes, frightened her for a long time. But knowing that it was the best painting in the show, she overcame her fear. In this statement one can hear the old Peggy—the flighty creature protesting that a picture almost scared her too much to buy—giving way to the more assured and confident Peggy, who admired the painting, however much it alarmed her. The exhibition was a success—critically, commercially, and esthetically—and Peggy was particularly pleased with the way in which the paintings were hung. While the show was up, Wyn Henderson rented a motor launch for a drunken party, during which there were many scenes "from various jealousies."

Tanguy was happy to have money for the first time in his life, but, despite the improvement in his finances, his modest and "adorable" personality remained unchanged. When he was drunk, which according to Peggy, was quite often, his hair stood straight up on his head. A fervent devotee of Breton's, he was committed to Surrealism. "It was worse than having a religion, and it governed all his actions, like Garman's Communism."

The pleasure Peggy took in the company of the unspoiled M. and Mme Tanguy did not stop her from seducing the painter. Though Peggy could be extremely possessive, she never seemed to feel that there was anything reprehensible about sleeping with other women's lovers and husbands. Not long before her affair with Tanguy, she had had a quick romance with Giorgio Joyce, whose wife, Helen, had been Peggy's friend since Peggy worked at the Sunwise Turn in New York, and who—at the time Peggy slept with Giorgio—was in the hospital, having suffered a nervous breakdown.

This was symptomatic of one of Peggy's most serious character flaws: a certain lack of empathy that kept her from understanding that others—her children, her lovers, her lovers' wives—might not feel the way she wished them to feel. Coupled with a certain inability to deny herself anything she wanted—be it a new painting, or a new man—this trait led her to fail the people she loved in ways that seem far more problematic than the flaws of which she was more often accused: promiscuity, shallowness, stinginess, and a sense of humor that sometimes crossed over into malice.

Emily Coleman, whose understanding of her friend was at once astute and generous, considered Peggy's principal failing to have been the self-absorption that prevented her from imagining the lives—and the probable emotional responses—of others. "She is as absorbed in herself as any human being I ever saw. I do at times concentrate on the lives of others, though I'm so egotistical. Peggy really cannot, although she believes she ought to. She cannot *think* of another person's life. This characteristic, which she deplores . . . seems to me to reveal that she is in some curious way an artist."

Peggy's affair with Tanguy began at a party given by the painter Roland Penrose, who owned the gallery that Mesens directed; Peggy and Tanguy left the gathering to be alone in Peggy's flat. Subsequent assignations were arranged with the help of Wyn Henderson, who distracted Tanguy's increasingly suspicious wife so that the lovers could meet. Like all of Peggy's romances, this one was tempestuous. During an intense argument, Peggy slipped and fell into her enormous fireplace, from which Tanguy rescued her before she was burned by the flames.

When the Tanguys returned to France, Peggy conspired to see Yves again. She arranged for her children, who were both staying with her at the time, to be taken care of. She caught a boat to France, where she met Tanguy and set off with him for Rouen. They then caught another ferry back to England. Peggy describes their "elopement" with no remorse or compassion for the unhappy Mme Tanguy; she reports with some amusement that Sindbad was puzzled to see the painter again, this time without his wife. In London, Tanguy read Proust (which appears to have become a sort of test that Peggy demanded of her lovers) but was impatient to return to Paris and see Breton.

In the midst of this, Beckett returned to fascinate and torment Peggy. Seeing a photo of her and Tanguy, he became jealous, and offered her the use of his flat in Paris, which she accepted—to spend time with Tanguy. Though Peggy "really liked [Mme Tanguy] and did not want to make her unhappy," she was at once horrified and entertained when, in a café, they ran into the painter's wife and she hurled three pieces of fish at Peggy. Meanwhile, Tanguy sensed that Peggy was still pining for Beckett, and he accused her of wanting to come to Paris to see Sam. Genuinely in love with Peggy, and grateful for her help in promoting his work, Tanguy gave her a cigarette lighter engraved with an erotic drawing and a pair of earrings painted with one of his signature lunar landscapes; later she would wear one of the earrings at the opening of her Art of This Century gallery in New York.

Back in London on the eve of the Munich conference, Peggy was afraid that war would be declared and that London and Paris would be bombed. In a panic, she arranged to have all the art in the gallery moved to Yew Tree Cottage. But when British Prime Minister Neville Chamberlain returned from Munich with his false assurances about the Germans' good intentions, Peggy returned to London and celebrated by mounting a show of children's art. Among the works on view was a painting of three naked men running up a flight of stairs, which had been done by Sigmund Freud's young grandson Lucian.

Pleased by how much of Tanguy's work was still selling, Peggy decided that Roland Penrose should buy a painting. In attempting to do Tanguy a favor, Peggy observed, she did him a disservice: she began an affair with Penrose, who liked to bind the wrists of his lovers. Once, Penrose used Peggy's belt; on another occasion he produced a pair of ivory handcuffs with a lock and key. Their romance was short-lived; Penrose was in love with the beautiful and gifted American photographer Lee Miller, who had left him to marry an Egyptian and live in Cairo. Peggy urged him to win back Lee, and she returned to Tanguy, who was dismayed to learn that Peggy had been unfaithful to him with Penrose.

Early in 1939, Peggy began to consider the idea of founding a museum of modern art in London. She convinced Herbert Read to be its first director, and promised him five years' salary in advance; Wyn Henderson was put on staff. Read told the British press that the museum, which he hoped would open in the fall of 1939, would include a permanent collection and temporary exhibitions not only of painting but of sculpture, music, and architecture, and would offer educational lectures and concerts. Hoping that she would be able to raise additional funds, Peggy designated a considerable amount of money for the project, and she set off for Paris to purchase more art.

But by autumn of that year, Hitler's invasion of Poland and the growing evidence of Germany's plan for world domination had made it clear that war was inevitable, and Peggy realized that her plans for the museum were impractical. Herbert Read was given a generous settlement—half of the five years' salary that he had been promised—to console him for the loss of the project, which he continued to believe was feasible. In June, Guggenheim Jeune mounted its final show—graphics by the British printmaker Stanley Hayter and paintings by Julian Trevelyan—then closed with a party on June 22.

In August 1939, Peggy and her friend Nellie van Doesburg —the widow of the painter Theo van Doesburg, a high-spirited and energetic woman who would remain Peggy's close friend well into old age—set off for Paris, where Peggy would use the money she had set aside for the London museum to finance her mission of buying a painting a day.

Paris Before the War

WHEN PEGGY and Nellie arrived in France, Peggy was in
a fragile state, and seemed to have lost some of the confidence
and resilience she'd developed as director of Guggenheim
Jeune. Tanguy had found another mistress, the American artist Kay Sage, and Peggy experienced his defection as a painful
rejection. Her health was weak, perhaps as a lingering consequence of an abortion she had undergone in early 1939. Peggy
and Nellie visited Megève, where they turned Sindbad over to
his father and stepmother, and where Kay Boyle's hatred for
Peggy appeared to be outliving her passion for Peggy's former
husband. From Megève, Peggy and Nellie continued on to the
south of France.

The signing of the Hitler-Stalin pact had dramatically increased the uncertainty and tension throughout Europe. Peggy
briefly considered taking the children to London. But Laurence

persuaded her to remain in France until they had a clearer sense of what was going to happen.

Peggy and Nellie decided to establish a refuge where artists could wait out the war; perhaps Peggy was envisioning a large communal household on the model of Hayford Hall. But her plans came to nothing. "Had I known more about artists at that time I would never have dreamt of anything so mad as trying to live with them in any kind of harmony or peace. . . . As soon as I got back to Paris and met a few of the people we had thought of inviting, I realized what a hell life would have been. They not only could not have lived together, but did not even want to come to dinner with each other."

Back in Paris, her energies restored, Peggy addressed the problem of what to do about Djuna Barnes. By now her friendship with Djuna (and Djuna's physical and mental condition) had so deteriorated that Peggy threatened to withdraw her support unless Barnes curbed her drinking. Enraged by the idea that Peggy was entertaining the idea of starting a museum while she was starving, Djuna wrote to Emily Coleman (who had moved to Arizona) that Peggy had gone mad like her forbears, and would surely have been locked up in an asylum were she not so wealthy. Eventually, Peggy arranged for Djuna Barnes and Yves Tanguy to sail on the same boat for the United States.

Peggy stayed first at Mary Reynolds's apartment, where she had spent her idyll with Beckett, who appeared in Peggy's life yet again—just in time to watch her fall down a flight of stairs and dislocate her knee, an injury that required a stay at the American Hospital. After her discharge, Peggy moved into Kay Sage's former apartment on the Île Saint-Louis.

Paris seemed safe for the moment, and Peggy took pleasure in the beauty of her home, in its proximity to the Seine, and in the fact that she could lie in bed and watch the play of the light on the river reflected on her ceiling. It was, Peggy writes, one of the happiest times in her life. She gave a lot of dinner parties, for which—assisted by Mary's maid—she did her own cooking.

Accompanied by Nellie van Doesburg, who disapproved of many of her choices and with whom she often disagreed, Peggy set out to buy a painting a day. As she rushed from studio to studio, from purchase to purchase, she was also assisted by one of her most influential advisers: an eccentric and somewhat mysterious man named Howard Putzel, who had run a gallery in Los Angeles and who had lent Peggy some Tanguy paintings for her show at Guggenheim Jeune. When Putzel arrived in Paris, Peggy was surprised to discover that he was not the "little black hunchback" she had imagined but rather "a big, fat blond." In his memoir, Jimmy Ernst describes Putzel as resembling "a well-worn teddy bear." Competitive and frequently in conflict with Nellie van Doesburg, Putzel encouraged and counseled Peggy as she continued her whirlwind spree, urging her to buy things she didn't want and others that he felt she needed in order to fill gaps and round out her collection.

One day, Gala Dalí dragged Peggy all over Paris, searching for one of her husband's paintings for Peggy to buy, all the time scolding Peggy for her foolishness in devoting herself to modern art when it was so much more practical (and more lucrative) to promote the career of one artist, as Gala had done and would continue to do. Predictably, the two women disliked each other despite (or because of) the traits they shared: intense social and professional ambition, a fierce independence, and a nervy refusal to let their sexuality and their personal lives be dictated by convention. Before meeting Dalí, Gala had lived in a ménage à trois with Max Ernst, whom Peggy would later marry. Later, Gala and Salvador would capitalize on what Peggy had done to bring modern art into the public eye, and would go much farther, staging publicity stunts and attention-grabbing events to further Dalí's career. When Peggy finally bought a painting entitled *The Birth of Liquid Desires* from Dalí, she claimed to have somehow failed to notice how sexual its subject matter was; that is difficult to imagine, given that almost half of the canvas is occupied by a pelvis, and at the center of the composition a naked man and woman embrace.

If Peggy's description of her marriage to Laurence Vail is among her memoir's more upsetting chapters, her account of her experiences acquiring art in prewar Paris is one of the less attractive. She makes her art-shopping bender sound like a series of skirmishes which she invariably won by holding her ground and waiting out the artists who knew that war was coming, who had no idea what would happen to them, and who wondered whether they would ever again see another buyer for their work—presuming their work survived. Peggy describes it as a game. Was this really true? Did she have second thoughts about the bargains she was getting, momentary pricks of conscience that would have seemed to her too dull and serious to include in the lively narrative of how she simultaneously outfoxed the Germans and put together a major art collection? Her memoir doesn't say. What does seem evident is that she had a limited budget with which to dispense her aid and her largesse, and that she genuinely believed that she was helping the artists.

Several pages of *Out of This Century* are devoted to the most hard-fought of these struggles: her battle to acquire Brancusi's *Bird in Space.* Peggy had long coveted the piece in which the Romanian sculptor had managed to combined stasis and motion, grace, flesh, and polished brass, takeoff and flight commingled with just enough gravity to stay upright and balanced. But she couldn't afford it. "Now the moment seemed to have arrived for this great acquisition." Though Peggy knew that Brancusi asked high prices for his work, she'd hoped that their "excessive friendship" might persuade him to be more reasonable. "But in spite of all this, we ended up in a terrible row, when he asked four thousand dollars for the *Bird in Space*."

Having embraced austerity, having sacrificed pleasure and comfort for the sake of his art, Brancusi—who slept in a small room upstairs from his studio and cooked delicious meals on his forge—had, in his old age, taken to combining high living with a taste for practical jokes. He enjoyed arriving in luxury hotels, dressed as a peasant and accompanied by young girls, and ordering from the top of the menu. He invited Peggy along on one of these excursions, but she declined. Together they would dress up and go out for dinner, "but though he loved me very much, I could never get anything out of him." Laurence suggested that Peggy marry Brancusi so she would inherit his sculpture, but she suspected (doubtless correctly) that the plan would fail.

One day, while Peggy and Brancusi were having lunch at his studio, the Germans launched an air raid on the outer boulevards of Paris. The sculptor insisted that Peggy move away from under the skylight, a suggestion with which she only partly complied. Afterward they went outside to learn that the city had been heavily bombed, and that many schoolchildren had been killed.

Several months after their argument over *Bird in Space*, Peggy sent Nellie to mollify Brancusi, who accepted Peggy's offer after some negotiation involving the differential provided by the relative values of the franc and the dollar.

The Germans were nearing Paris when Peggy arrived to claim her sculpture, which Brancusi had been polishing by hand. Peggy professed not to know why the sculptor was unhappy to sell his masterpiece for a fraction of what it was worth. "Tears were streaming down Brancusi's face, and I was genuinely touched. I never knew why he was so upset, but assumed it was because he was parting with his favorite bird."

It was through Howard Putzel that Peggy met Max Ernst, whose work she admired and whose good looks impressed her even as his reserve impelled her to chatter on, in order to fill the awkward silences that punctuated her visit to his studio. With him was his lover, the much younger Leonora Carrington. Writing after the end of her marriage to Ernst, Peggy could not resist making the catty observation that Max and Leonora resembled Little Nell and her grandfather in Dickens's *The Old Curiosity Shop.*

Ernst was legendary for his physical beauty. Decades later, when Michael Wishart met him at Peggy's palazzo in Venice, time seemed not to have dimmed the painter's appeal:

> Tanned, leathery, with a delicate skeleton and a prominent beak-like nose, his obsession with birds was immediately understandable. He also had large ferociously penetrating eyes suggesting the amazing observation of a sparrowhawk. I have met only two other people with this very intense gaze, Picasso and Francis Bacon. It is a curious coincidence that three of the greatest painters of our time should share this physical attribute with birds of prey. Max had the exquisite formal manners of a German baron in a movie, and a quick wit.

Though Peggy had gone to Ernst's Paris studio intending to purchase one of his paintings, she wound up (after Putzel told her that the Ernsts were "too cheap") buying one of Carrington's. This decision must have haunted her when, only a short time later, she became emotionally entangled with Max and Leonora.

That spring, Peggy drove to Megève to pick up Sindbad and Pegeen for a skiing trip to the Alps. While the children skied, Peggy had an affair with a "perfectly horrible" but handsome Italian she met in the hotel. On her return to Megève, Peggy again fell down the stairs, hurting her ankle and elbow.

Though it would be been wiser to recuperate in Megève, the animosity between Peggy and Kay was still so bitter that, though injured, Peggy chose to drive back to Paris rather than stay with Laurence and Kay.

In the capital, where there was growing concern about the coming war, Peggy continued to acquire art; she purchased a painting and several photographs from Man Ray. The narrowness of her focus provoked an argument with Mary Reynolds, who accused Peggy of being so fixated on her collection that, if she found a truck to transport it, she would happily run down any refugees who had the misfortune to get in her way.

Hurt but undeterred by her friend's accusation, Peggy rented an apartment on the Place Vendôme where (choosing to ignore the realities of the historical moment) she planned to start a museum in which to show her collection; part of what attracted her to the romantic site was the fact that Chopin had died in one of its rooms. She immediately began remodeling and modernizing the décor to provide a more suitable setting.

At the last minute, she awoke from her fantasy about the future and decided to ship her collection out of Paris. Recalling this time, Peggy focused on the generosity of the landlord, who removed all the fin de siècle angels and ornaments without Peggy having signed a lease or paid a deposit on the Place Vendôme apartment. "After I left Paris, I had a bad conscience and sent him twenty thousand francs indemnity. I have never known such a landlord." And so the landlord's kindness stirred the remorse that all of Brancusi's tears failed to awaken.

After hearing that the Louvre wouldn't shelter her collection, Peggy arranged to have it stored in the barn on the grounds of her friend Marie Jolas's school near Vichy. Peggy was reluctant to leave the capital, where she had begun an affair with a man named Bill Whidney: "We used to sit in cafes and drink champagne. It is really incomprehensible now to think of our idiotic life, when there was so much misery surrounding us.

Trains kept pouring into Paris with refugees in the direst misery and with bodies that had been machine-gunned en route. I can't imagine why I didn't go to the aid of all these unfortunate people. But I just didn't; instead I drank champagne with Bill."

Discovering that her travel permit had expired, Peggy tried and was unable to renew it. Her anxiety grew, fueled by a nightmare in which she was trapped in Paris.

Sex had become, for Peggy, not only a source of pleasure and excitement but an analgesic that alleviated her fear. During these last months before the German invasion, when some part of her knew that she would have to leave Europe, even as she pretended (to herself and others) that things might somehow go on as they had before, she took a succession of casual lovers, among them the married Bill Whidney and the "horrible" but handsome Italian with whom she flirted when Pegeen and Sindbad skied.

Three days before the Germans entered Paris, Nellie, Peggy, and her two Persian cats left the city in her blue Talbot convertible, its trunk filled with the canisters of hoarded gasoline. Though the horrors of the mass exodus from Paris, along roads that were strafed by German planes, are by now widely known, Peggy recalled it as a lark. "It was terrific."

Their progress was slow at first as they crept along the route to Fontainebleau, which was jammed with refugees carrying their belongings. But the traffic soon thinned out. Most people were headed south, toward Bordeaux, while Peggy—despite warnings that she would encounter the Italian army—drove east toward Megève, where her children were safe with Laurence and Kay.

Laurence believed that they should avoid the chaos of the French roads, remain in Megève, and see how the situation developed. Peggy agreed to wait, as Laurence suggested, until they were sure that they would have to leave Europe. Relaxing at Lac d'Annecy, she resolved to have an affair with a member of the lower class, a hot romance out of D. H. Lawrence. She soon found a hairdresser who appears to have had more talent as a lover than in his chosen profession. Peggy's efforts to keep her romance a secret necessitated spending a great deal of time in the salon, where she had her hair dyed a different color every few weeks and where she persuaded Pegeen to get an unflattering permanent wave.

By now, Sindbad was seventeen, his sister two years younger. During the school term, Sindbad had been attending Bedales, a progressive boarding school in Hampshire, with boys whom Michael Wishart, also a student there, described as "pleasant, alien, masturbating louts." At Bedales, discipline ranged from lax to nonexistent; Wishart was allowed to skip his classes if he pretended to be in "a coma of inspiration" in front of his easel. Sindbad chose to play games, especially cricket, of which he was fond, a passion his mother found impossible to comprehend.

Pegeen remained more artistic, an inclination that Peggy had always encouraged. It is impossible to know and pointless to speculate about how much of Pegeen's desire to paint was innate or genuine, how much was the natural result of growing up around artists, and how much represented an attempt to snag the attention of a neglectful or distracted mother whose love for (and interest in) art and men was often more compelling than her maternal feelings.

That summer, Pegeen and Sindbad (along with their stepsiblings) found themselves the subject of the grown-ups' playful—and intrusive—inquisitions into their sex lives. For Peggy, Laurence, and their friends, this was another way of distinguishing themselves from repressed bourgeois society, and—especially when large amounts of alcohol had been consumed—it seemed amusing to chatter on about sex in the presence of the young. Had they lost their virginity, and if not, when would they?

Complicating matters for the troubled brother and sister was the fact that, during their stay at Lac d'Annecy, Peggy and her children became closely involved with a French-American family, the Kuhns, who lived nearby. Sindbad fell in love with the Kuhns' daughter, Pegeen became infatuated with their son, and Peggy herself had a brief and comical dalliance—like something out of a French farce—with the wife's brother, who had just escaped from a prison camp. Peggy's account of her romances that summer—with the hairdresser and with the "uncle" next door—makes it seem as if she had begun to regard every new landscape as a vista to be scanned for a viable sexual partner.

At the end of the summer, Peggy and Nellie moved to Grenoble, and Peggy traveled frequently to Marseilles, where she became involved with—and aided—the Emergency Rescue Committee. Varian Fry's skill in raising money was evidenced by the fact that he approached Peggy with the idea of saving André Breton, arguably the most powerful of the Surrealists, together with his family and his doctor. Rescuing the Bretons was a worthy cause, and Peggy could hardly refuse to help a founding father of the movement whose work she had championed, exhibited—and sold. Peggy agreed to finance the Bretons' passage to the United States, but she drew the line at paying to get his doctor out of Europe.

Peggy's generosity helped assure her welcome at Air-Bel, the spacious, ramshackle nineteenth-century villa on the outskirts of Marseilles where Fry housed the refugee artists while he and his coworkers completed the massive paperwork required to leave France, cross the Iberian Peninsula, and enter the United States. "In order to get an exit visa, one first needed affidavits of support and sponsorship from respondents in the host country, along with an entry visa from the country's government (no small feat if the destination was America). In addition, transit visas had to be obtained for every stop en route;

and the boats out were so few and seldom that even if one managed to obtain all the appropriate visas, by the time transportation could be booked one of them had expired, or one's money had run out, or both."

With Breton at its center, the social life at Air-Bel was a round-the-clock Surrealist happening, with elements reminiscent of Peggy's summers at Hayford Hall. In the evenings, the residents talked about sex, read aloud from Surrealist texts, and played games that included Truth or Consequences, Exquisite Corpse, and a popular entertainment entitled Who Would You Most Like to See Dead? Breton produced a table centerpiece made from a bottle in which live praying mantises mated and devoured one another.

Yet despite the artists' efforts to remain optimistic and productive, their worries—and the dangers—were increasing. In December 1940, in advance of Marshal Pétain's official visit to Marseilles, a squad of plainclothes police arrived at Air-Bel, searched the rooms, and arrested the residents. Because the city's jails were full, the artists and their families were kept in a ship docked offshore. Breton was thrown into the ship's hold along with Varian Fry. They were detained there for four days and were released only when the Vichy leader's tour of the port city had ended without incident.

In the winter of 1941, Max Ernst—who had just gotten out of prison camp—arrived to stay at Air-Bel, where he was welcomed by his fellow artists, who knew and admired his work. And it was there that Peggy again met the painter whose studio she had visited during her manic art-buying tour of Paris.

In a 1936 essay, Max Ernst discussed himself in the third person: "Women find it difficult to reconcile the gentleness and moderation of what he says with the tranquil violence of his ideas. They liken him to an earthquake: but an earthquake so well-behaved that it hardly moves the furniture around. . . . What is particularly disagreeable to them—what they can't bear, in fact—is that they cannot put their fingers on WHAT HE IS. . . . The ladies describe him . . . as a monster who loves to turn landscape upside down."

In his book on Ernst, John Russell remarks that the real subject of this passage is "the artist's equilibrium between opposing forces within his nature, and that that equilibrium must be brought out by means partly conscious and partly unconscious." While this is probably true, the fact remains that when a writer talks about "women" and "ladies," we must assume that he is at least partly talking about "women" and "ladies."

By the time Max and Peggy became involved, everyone in their circle seemed to have known that Ernst had left his second wife, Marie-Berthe, for Leonora Carrington, who had gone mad during the most recent of Ernst's prison internments and was currently in a mental asylum. Carrington was famous not only for her beauty but for her talent and wit; she enjoyed a respect that the Surrealists rarely afforded women. At an elegant restaurant, she had blithely slathered her feet with mustard while chatting with her fellow guests, a Surrealist act that impressed even André Breton, who called Carrington "superb in her refusals, with a boundless human authenticity."

All this was known to Peggy at Max's fiftieth birthday party, when she and Max conducted their two-sentence courtship: *When can we meet again? Tomorrow at four at the Café de la Paix and you know why.*

There is very little about Peggy Guggenheim's romances with men that can make one feel sanguine about her character, her emotional stability, her luck, or the possibility of honest and loving relationships between women and men. By 1941, Peggy was no longer a naïve, sheltered girl willing to accept whatever humiliation Laurence Vail intuited that she would endure. At forty-three, she had already run a successful London gallery and spent tens of thousands of dollars on building a collection of modern art. She had two children, close friends, money, and a mission.

But when she fell in love with Max Ernst, she embarked on an affair as demeaning as any in her youth. Initially intrigued, Max Ernst stayed with Peggy for her money, for her willingness to facilitate his escape from Europe, for security, and later for her ability to help him become established in the United States. Years later, people who knew Peggy—the art historians Rosamund Bernier and John Richardson—would remark, as if it were a fact known to all, that Max's interest in Peggy was ultimately financial.

With her gift for ignoring what she chose not to see, Peggy fell more deeply under Max's spell. When she brought him to Megève, Pegeen and Sindbad (doubtless grateful for some distraction from watching their father's marriage to Kay Boyle disintegrate just as they were about to leave the continent where they had spent their lives) were charmed by Max's mystique, his cape, and his courtly manners. But even the two teenagers soon figured out the truth about their mother's boyfriend's intentions.

Peggy knew that Max would only bring her grief, just as she knew that she would have to leave Europe, just as she knew that she could no longer travel in France because she was a Jew, just as she knew (without needing Max to tell her) why the police's visit to her hotel room in Marseilles could have gone so drastically wrong, just as she knew that the forged signature on her visa was a problem, just as she knew that it was going to take a lot of work and some luck to get Max Ernst and her family out of France and safely to the United States.

New York

No ONE expected the trip to be easy. Max Ernst was detained at the Spanish border and would have been arrested had not a sympathetic French guard indicated which of the two trains waiting at the station was headed for Spain: that was the train which Ernst was forbidden to take, and which he promptly boarded. The group—Peggy and Ernst, Kay and Laurence, and the children—were reunited in Lisbon, where Kay checked into a hospital, claiming a sinus infection in order to be spared the theatrics generated by her soon-to-be ex-husband, his ex-wife, the ex-wife's lover, and Leonora, the lover of the ex-wife's lover, who had inconveniently—and dramatically—reentered their lives.

Max had met Peggy at the station in Lisbon with the news that Carrington had turned up, released from the asylum and in the company of a Mexican diplomat whom she (to Max's horror) was planning to marry. Max made no effort to hide the fact that he was still in love with Leonora. Peggy and her children took rooms in a hotel, while Laurence and Kay and their daughters boarded at the pension where Max was staying as he tried to sort out his feelings.

Peggy was so upset (not only was she in love with Ernst but she was financing and arranging his passage to the United States) that she contemplated marrying an Englishman she had met on the train from France; maybe she should follow him to England and get a war job. Laurence convinced her that, no matter what Max did, it would be cruel to abandon the children in this hazardous and uncertain situation.

One night, everyone (including the Mexican diplomat) went out dancing. It was, Peggy reports, "a mad evening, full of terrible scenes."

Soon after, Leonora married her Mexican fiancé and went into the hospital for an operation on her breast. Max visited her often, and Peggy envied the companionable happiness that Max and Leonora shared as they sat in silence and drew. In her memoir, Peggy describes how struck she was by Leonora's beauty and in particular by her "tip-tilted nose," the nose for which Peggy had longed all her life and that she had tried to acquire in Cincinnati. As Leonora vacillated between returning to Max and leaving with her Mexican husband, Kay Boyle helped convince her that living with Max would mean resuming the servile and submissive role that Leonora had outgrown, the one positive side effect of her sufferings during Max's prison term.

Thrown into close quarters with the adults, the children were again disconcerted to find their sex lives becoming the topic of their parents' conversation. Sindbad was obsessed with losing his virginity, but his mother urged him not to do so with any of the local women, because venereal disease was rampant in Lisbon. Pegeen's friend Jacqueline Ventadour, who was traveling with them, was in love with Sindbad, but he remained faithful to the girl he'd courted the previous summer at Lac d'Annecy, Yvonne Kuhn, the brother of Pegeen's lover.

One night Peggy swam naked off the beach at Cascais. According to Peggy, Max was terrified that if she drowned, there would be no one to help him reach the United States: not precisely the sort of anxiety one might hope for from a lover. When she emerged from the sea, they made love on rocks that turned out to be the village latrine. "Max loved my unconventionalities," Peggy concluded.

At last they boarded the luxurious Pan Am Clipper, equipped with salons and a dining room but, inconveniently, one berth too few for Peggy's party. Max was given Pegeen's bed, and Pegeen was obliged to bunk with her mother—thus initiating one of many struggles that Max, Peggy, and Pegeen would wage for space and power.

Throughout Peggy's relationship with Max, she and Max and Pegeen fought bitterly and often, forming, breaking, and reforging alliances, two of them siding against the third, competing for love and attention. It was a challenge for Max to overlook the beauty of his unloved lover's teenage daughter, just as it would have been hard for Pegeen, now a sentient adolescent, to see her mother humiliate herself by alternately being difficult and begging Max to love her. There was an element of eroticism, or at least suppressed flirtation, in the relationship between Max and Pegeen. One need only look at the way Pegeen appears as a forlorn and beautiful figure in Max's painting, *The Antipope:* a painting that would cause Peggy great pain.

The plane stopped in the Azores for refueling, and again in the Bermudas. On Bastille Day, 1941, Peggy (wearing the enormous sombrero she'd bought in the Azores) and her party landed at LaGuardia Marine Air Terminal in New York. Also on board was a scientist importing a cargo of experimental rodents, inspiring the headline "8 Guinea Pigs Here by Clipper Travel."

The new arrivals were greeted by Howard Putzel and by Max's son Jimmy, a painter then working in the mailroom of the Museum of Modern Art. Of all the literary portraits of Peggy that exist, Jimmy Ernst's memoir, *A Not-So-Still Life*, includes one of the most sympathetic and (along with Emily Coleman's diary and Gregory Corso's letters) the most evocative account of what it was like to spend time in Peggy's company.

Having observed the damage caused by his father's relationships with women, Jimmy Ernst had reason to sympathize with Peggy. His own mother, Lou Straus-Ernst, Max's first wife, had been abandoned in Europe (partly because she refused to pretend to Varian Fray that she and Ernst were still married) and was to die in Auschwitz. Max was by no means a warm or attentive father. According to Peggy, Jimmy longed to be close to Max, but his presence made Max uncomfortable, and Max didn't know how to talk to his son. Moved by Jimmy's plight, Peggy "became a sort of stepmother to him." and felt more comfortable with Jimmy than she did with Max.

Watching Peggy arrive at LaGuardia, Jimmy was struck by her vulnerability. "The anxiety-ridden eyes were warm and almost pleading, and the bony hands, at a loss where to go, moved like ends of broken windmills around an undisciplined coiffure of dark hair. There was something about her that made me want to reach out to her, even before she spoke." When she did speak, it was to tell Jimmy more than he wanted to know about the people with whom she was traveling, and also to ask whether Max had told his son—or anyone—about his relationship with her. Max hadn't.

Traveling on a German passport, Max Ernst was instantly apprehended by U.S. immigration officials. Since the day's last ferry across New York Bay to the alien detention center had left, three officers followed Max to his hotel and, the next day, took him to Ellis Island, where he was imprisoned. Peggy called Jimmy to reassure him that the people vouching for Max—

Nelson Rockefeller, Eleanor Roosevelt, John Hay Whitney—would soon secure his release. On July 17, Jimmy was called to testify at a hearing. Though he earned only sixty dollars a month at the museum and lived in a furnished room, Jimmy was directed to sign a paper swearing that he would assume financial responsibility for his father, and Max was allowed to go free.

On the ferry to Manhattan, Jimmy watched the artists and dignitaries who had (unnecessarily, as it turned out) come to testify on Max's behalf crowd around his father. Even as Jimmy hoped that Max might have given up his obsession with beautiful girls and would be loyal or simply kind to this "shy and ungainly woman [who] felt herself to be part of Max's life," he watched Max and his supporters drive off to a celebration at the Belmont Plaza Hotel and completely forget about Jimmy and Peggy, leaving them to share a cab. "Peggy tried to maintain her poise at this insensitive slight with rapid intakes of breath and a simultaneous twitching of her head." Once more, Peggy rattled on about her family and her children and tried to find out whether Max had mentioned her to Jimmy. *Had he said anything about her at all?*

Writes Jimmy Ernst, "I was bewildered and touched. Sophisticated and mature people were not supposed to be so insecure. ... Was Peggy telling me something of herself? A lifetime of uncertainty concerning the motives of anyone within the vicinity of her feelings?"

At the party, Peggy grabbed Jimmy's arm when André Breton asked Max when Leonora was arriving. Max changed the subject and was uncharacteristically affectionate to Peggy to make clear his situation. Peggy showed that no harm had been done, no offense taken, by offering Breton two hundred dollars a month for a year, in order to smooth his transition to life in the United States. She was heartened when Howard Putzel informed her that her collection had arrived safely and was waiting to clear customs.

As she left the celebration, Peggy asked Jimmy to be her secretary. She offered him twenty-five dollars a week, in return for which he would run errands, write letters, keep records, and catalogue the collection. Jimmy accepted, though he feared that he was risking an "unreasoning involvement" in "the vagaries of my father's personal life." Jimmy, wrote Peggy, "was efficient and bright and knew everything, and I loved him and we got on marvelously."

During their early, comparatively carefree days in New York, Peggy and Max visited the Museum of Modern Art, which was staging a major Picasso exhibition. The museum's director, Alfred H. Barr, Jr., who was to become a cherished friend of Peggy's and another of her advisers, took them to see the cellar, where Ernst's paintings were stored, along with a "pretty fine" collection of "Picassos, Braques, Légers, Dalís, Rousseaus, Arps, Tanguys, and Calders, but not one Kandinksky."

Peggy's response to the museum itself was already that of a competitor: "The atmosphere of the whole place was that of a girls' college. Yet at the same time it looked rather like a millionaire yacht club." Peggy was even less charitable about her uncle's collection: "It really was a joke. There were a few excellent paintings, and almost a hundred by Bauer," the lover of Baroness Rebay, Solomon Guggenheim's mistress. "From the walls boomed forth music by Bach—a rather weird contrast. The museum itself was a beautiful little building completely wasted in this atrocious manner." Peggy also visited her uncle's private collection, a marvelous assortment of modern paintings hung in the Plaza Hotel suite occupied by Peggy's Aunt Irene.

Jimmy's fears about his father's behavior soon proved justified. Leonora Carrington arrived in New York with a cache of Max's work, and their brief reunion was a source of anguish for Max—and Peggy. Peggy was devastated when Max gave her a book signed with the inscription, "To Peggy Guggenheim from Max Ernst"—notably cool, she felt, compared with the declarations of undying love and passion with which Max inscribed books to Leonora. The daily crises between Max and Peggy complicated Jimmy's job, which at that point mostly involved fielding requests for charity donations and patronage, as he and Peggy looked for a place in which to show her collection.

Max's refusal to stop seeing Leonora was so distressing that Peggy threatened to leave him, then decided to visit the West Coast, where she planned to look for a place, far from New York (and Leonora), to locate her gallery-museum. She and Max, Jimmy, and Pegeen flew to California. In Santa Monica, they stayed with Peggy's sister Hazel and rejected a range of sites—Charles Laughton's former mansion, a bowling alley, adobe churches, a garage that had once belonged to Ramón Novarro—as possible homes for her art. She also visited and admired Walter Arensberg's collection of modern art, which Duchamp had helped Arensberg assemble.

Eventually, Peggy decided that California was the wrong place for her—and her collection. As they drove back east, Peggy, Max, and Pegeen argued constantly. In Arizona, the mother and daughter made an arduous trip to visit Emily Coleman, who was living with her cowboy lover in "unspeakable squalor" on an isolated ranch. When Peggy took Emily to meet Max, the two got along, but Emily told Peggy "how much I showed my insecurity with him, and that pained me. I had hoped to hide it."

Each time they crossed a state border, Peggy sent Jimmy to find out about that state's legal requirements for obtaining a marriage license, a quest that infuriated Max, who didn't want to get married. Though Peggy joked about her reluctance to "live in sin with an enemy alien," she had been alarmed by her powerlessness to help Max at LaGuardia and Ellis Island, and she hoped that marriage would give him (a German in a country that would soon declare war on Germany) a more secure foothold in the United States.

Back in New York, Peggy found a grand and beautiful apartment, a triplex known as Hale House, on East 51st Street overlooking the East River. It was large enough for Peggy to display some of her collection, for Max to have a studio, for Pegeen to have her own room, and for Jimmy to have an "office"—a two-story ballroom in which his duties involved the daily polishing of Brancusi's *Bird in Space*. Almost immediately, Peggy began giving lavish parties; regular guests included the stripper Gypsy Rose Lee, the writer William Saroyan, and a wide assortment of artists and critics, two of whom—Charles Henri Ford and Nicolas Calas—got into a fight so violent that Jimmy Ernst had to rescue the Kandinskys from being spattered with blood. Hale House became the site of more or less perpetual revelry, which only widened the gap between Max and Peggy.

> We never had a moment's peace in that wonderful place. Peace was the one thing Max needed in order to paint, and love was the one thing I needed in order to live. As neither of us gave the other what he most desired, our union was doomed to failure.

Throughout the fall of 1941 and the following winter, Peggy searched for space for her gallery, worked on the catalogue of her collection, and continued to buy the paintings and sculpture that, she felt, would fill its gaps. In the seven months between her return to New York and the completion of her catalogue, Peggy embarked on another buying spree almost as intense as the one that had preceded her departure from Europe; during this time she acquired seventy works of art. Some were bought directly from the artists; others, including several Joseph Cornell boxes, were located with the aid of Marcel Duchamp, while still others were purchased from the modern art galleries then operating in New York, run by dealers including Pierre Matisse, Julien Levy, Valentine Dudensing, and Karl Nierendorf.

According to Jimmy Ernst, the best paintings Peggy acquired during this period came from Max's studio, though these often caused Peggy as much anguish as pleasure. Many of the women that Ernst depicted and set in his lush, overgrown landscapes resembled Leonora, while Peggy made rare appearances as a female ogre. "It was painful for Peggy to recognize herself thusly and, during quiet moments in our work together, when she plaintively asked to be told that she was mistaken, I simply had to evade the question." Max painted Leonora over and over, and Peggy "was jealous that he never painted me. In fact it was a cause of great unhappiness to me and proof that he did not love me."

Tensions at home escalated, and Peggy argued with Max over subjects that ranged from Pegeen's charge account to Sindbad's sexuality to the price of lamb chops to the cost of indulging Max's passion for collecting Native American art, an obsession that had begun on their trip through the Southwest. They fought when Max borrowed the scissors with which John Holms had cut his beard. They fought over who drove the car. Max was frequently unfaithful to Peggy, obliging Jimmy to hide his father's affairs from a boss who was also his friend and later his stepmother.

For months, Peggy and Max quarreled about whether to get married. The question became more urgent after the Japanese attack on Pearl Harbor, when the United States entered the war and Peggy's joke about not wanting to live with an enemy alien was no longer remotely funny. On a visit to Peggy's cousin Harold Loeb in Washington, D.C., Peggy and Max were married by a judge in Virginia. But though marriage provided Peggy with a greater sense of safety, it failed to stop the couple's fights, battles that often lasted for days.

Peggy and Max had another scare when Peggy sent Max and Pegeen up to Cape Cod to stay with Matta and look for a summer house to rent. When Peggy arrived, she rejected the house they'd chosen, just in time for the FBI to drive up and arrest Max. They accused him of being a spy and tried to persuade him to denounce Matta; they charged him with having a shortwave radio, an illegal possession for an alien. They let him go but continued to harass him until one day they told Max that he had to go to Boston for a court hearing. Only after they got back to New York, and Peggy's accountant intervened, was the case against Max dismissed.

Leonora often called and asked Max to take her to lunch. Afterward, they would wander the city together—which Max never did with Peggy. She describes feeling hurt whenever she found him wearing his street clothes, which he never wore when he painted at home; his being dressed signified that he was going out with Leonora.

For much of her life, Peggy had insisted on her right to sleep with whomever she pleased, regardless of whether she or her lover was married or romantically involved with someone else. Now it was her turn to suffer because her husband was obsessed with another woman. Once, Peggy, Max, and Leonora had lunch with Djuna Barnes, who said that it was the only time she'd seen Max show any emotion. Leonora's presence had humanized him. "Otherwise he was as cold as a snake."

Peggy decided to test a long-standing mutual sexual attraction with Marcel Duchamp and in the process, she hoped, make Max jealous. One night, at dinner with Max and Marcel, Peggy got drunk, changed into a transparent green silk raincoat, and "ran around the house egging Marcel on. Max asked Marcel if he wanted me and of course he had to say no. To make matters worse I said the most terrible and insulting things to Max. Max began beating me violently, and Marcel looked on with his usual detached air, not interfering in any way."

Desperation inspired, in Peggy, a predilection for elaborate sexual acting-out. One night, she suggested that Max, Duchamp, John Cage, and his wife, Xenia (the Cages were staying with Peggy at Hale House), undress, and they would see who could keep from becoming aroused, a game that backfired when Max looked at the lovely Xenia—and visibly lost.

As the search for a gallery space continued, Peggy made progress on her catalogue. Max created a cover, and Breton assembled much of the text. Laurence Vail translated the foreign manuscripts, and above the image of one of his collages, contributed a revealing and touching statement: "I used to throw bottles and now I decorate them." There are prefaces by Breton, Arp, and Mondrian, an essay on Brancusi by Alfred H. Barr, Jr., a long essay on Surrealism by Max Ernst, poems by Paul Éluard and Charles Henri Ford, and remarkable statements on art accompanying photographs of paintings and sculpture by artists including Braque, Picasso, Kandinsky, Dalí, Calder, Delaunay, Miró, Gris, Carrington, Giacometti, Magritte, Man Ray, Malevich, Archipenko, Duchamp, Klee, and Henry Moore.

It was Breton's idea to depict each artist not with a full photo portrait but with a photo of his eyes. To Peggy's "great surprise," *Art of This Century* became more of an anthology than a straightforward exhibition catalogue. Paging through it, the reader is struck by the range and size of her collection, by the masterpieces it contained, and by the intelligence of many of her choices.

Dedicated to the memory of John Ferrar Holms, the book begins with three epigraphs. Of the two by Herbert Read, one refers to a "vital" and "experimental" art, currently in transition; the second explains the failure of Fascism to inspire great art because the spiritual activity required for artistic creation "works only in the plenitude of freedom." Sandwiched between these quotes is one from Adolf Hitler, who describes the "corruption of taste" displayed in the art that the Nazis termed degenerate, "pictures with green skies and purple seas . . . paintings which could only be explained by abnormal eyesight or willful fraud on the part of the painter. If they really paint in this manner because they see things this way, then these unhappy persons should be dealt with in the department of the Ministry of the Interior where sterilization is dealt with, to prevent them from passing on their unfortunate inheritance."

The obvious irony is that the catalogue contains the art that Hitler is describing. That Peggy included this quotation suggests that she and Breton were well aware of their historical moment, and of the fact that rescuing and showing Peggy's collection was a political gesture. The quotation from Hitler, in this context, may remind us of Peggy's delight when the hotel that excluded Jews burned down; another small victory had been scored against the enemies of the Jews and, in this case, of art.

In early 1942, Peggy found an exhibition space: two contiguous lofts on the top floor of a commercial building at 30 West 57th Street. She decided to name the gallery after the catalogue, *Art of This Century*. And she resolved to open a showcase for art unlike any that ever had existed.

Art of This Century

NOT LONG after returning from California, Peggy met Frederick Kiesler, the Vienna-trained modernist architect and polymath who had made his reputation as a designer of avant-garde art exhibitions and stage sets in Austria, Berlin, and Paris. In this country he had designed the Eighth Street Playhouse, done window displays for Saks Fifth Avenue, and been a professor of stagecraft at Juilliard. He and Peggy moved in the same social circles, and Kiesler was liked and admired by the people Peggy trusted most: Breton, Duchamp, Jimmy Ernst, and Howard Putzel.

In February 1942, Peggy wrote to Kiesler, asking his advice on turning "two tailor shops into an Art Gallery." Soon after, Peggy hired Kiesler to draw up the plans for combining the two lofts on West 57th. Kiesler's preliminary sketches made it clear that Art of This Century would be something new, a departure from the more conventional spaces—the Museum of Modern Art and Solomon Guggenheim's Museum of Non-Objective Painting—that Peggy found so uninspired.

Almost from the beginning, the professional relationship between Peggy Guggenheim and Frederick Kiesler was exciting, productive, and combative. They often argued over money. Peggy insisted that the building costs required to execute Kiesler's plans exceeded the budget that she had specified and could afford, though there is evidence that this was not the case, that his initial estimates and the final tally were closer than Peggy claimed.

Beneath these surface disagreements ran a deeper conflict. Peggy feared, and would continue to fear, that Kiesler's design would overshadow her collection, that her gallery would be noticed and remembered more for the way it had looked than for the masterpieces it contained. Peggy took consolation against the possibility in her memoir: "If the pictures suffered from the fact that their setting was too spectacular and took people's attention away from them, it was at least a marvelous decor and created a terrific stir."

Happily, Peggy and Kiesler agreed on a few important things: Art of This Century would combine a permanent installation —in effect, a museum—with a gallery featuring temporary exhibitions and works for sale. Everything possible would be done to subvert the traditional approach to exhibiting art. The setting would reflect the esthetics and theory of the art movements— Surrealism, Dadaism, Cubism, and Abstraction—represented in Peggy's collection. And it would change the way that people looked at art. No longer a passive spectator, the gallerygoer would have a cerebral and sensory *experience*.

The recollections of those who visited Art of This Century make it clear that not even the most telling photographs or the most eloquent descriptions can convey the excitement of what it was like to be there. Nor can we imagine how the gallery appeared to viewers who (like those fortunate enough to attend the 1938 Surrealist Exposition in Paris) had not yet been exposed to installations and happenings. We can only imagine how Kiesler's design would have astonished people whose encounters with art had been limited to traditional galleries and museums, with their ornate frames, subdued lighting, subtle wallpaper, venues in which masterpieces were hung to create the impression that one had wandered into the living room of a wealthy collector.

Most commercial galleries then, like their counterparts today, were designed to suggest that buying paintings was either a sign of belonging or an admission ticket to the rarefied cultural milieu. Meanwhile, the downtown, artist-run galleries weren't intended to be *fun*, but, rather, serious showplaces for the esthetics of one movement or another.

Not until Art of This Century did it occur to Americans that a gallery could be a cross between an amusement park, a haunted house, and a Paris café. According to Robert Motherwell, whose work was shown in Art of This Century's temporary exhibition space, the Daylight Gallery, "It seemed to me that part of the intention was to desanctify art, and treat it more like, say, books in the reading room of a library." At the same time, Peggy's gallery was envisioned as a temple of Modern Art, consecrated by the likes of Marcel Duchamp, André Breton, and Max Ernst.

The two lofts were joined and divided into four areas that could be easily reconfigured. In the Abstract and Cubist gallery, the floors were painted turquoise blue and the walls constructed of ultramarine canvas attached to the floors and ceilings so that the walls undulated and billowed like dark sails. Though the paintings appeared to be unframed, in fact Kiesler designed frames so slender as to be nearly invisible. The paintings were mounted at eye level on rope pulleys, triangular webbings that made them seem to float in space.

In the crepuscular Surrealist gallery, the walls were curved and the paintings hung on thick poles with brackets that allowed them to be tilted by the viewer. Played at regular intervals, a recording made it sound as if a locomotive were rushing through the room, and lights were set on timers to shine on first one part of the room, then—three seconds later—another. (The lighting system was abandoned for being too distracting and making it hard to see the paintings.)

In the Kinetic Gallery, Klee paintings were set along a conveyor belt. Pushing a button could bring a new one into view or halt the mechanism. By turning a large wheel, one could see Duchamp's *Boite-en-valise*, which featured reproductions he'd made of his own work. Closest to 57th Street, the white walls of the Daylight Gallery provided the venue for monthlong shows of the work of well-known and less established artists.

Art of This Century opened on October 20, 1942. The event was staged as a benefit for the American Red Cross; tickets cost a dollar. Alfred Barr lent Jimmy Ernst the Museum of Modern Art's list of members of the press who should receive invitations and information.

Peggy attended the glamorous party in a specially made white evening dress, wearing one earring designed by Alexander Calder, the other by Yves Tanguy—jewelry that signified her impartiality between Abstraction and Surrealism.

Widely publicized, cheered on by the press, the public, and the critics, Art of This Century became a cultural landmark and a tourist attraction: something that had to be seen. Celebrities arranged visits to coincide with special exhibits. A show called "The Negro in American Life," part of a citywide celebration of Harlem Week in association with the Council Against Intolerance in America, brought out the first lady, Eleanor Roosevelt, who praised the show in her newspaper column but declined Peggy's invitation to visit the Surrealist Gallery. "She retired through the door sideways, like a crab, pleading her ignorance of modern art." Dressed in her folkloric costume,

Frida Kahlo visited the gallery when her work was included in a show of women artists; Georgia O'Keeffe appeared at the gallery to announce her refusal to participate in a show of women artists.

Alfred Barr, Jr., and the architect Philip Johnson frequently stopped by. Mary McCarthy—one of the new women friends Peggy had made in New York—visited on occasion, and once Robert Motherwell brought Jean-Paul Sartre. The celebrity stripper Gypsy Rose Lee, who, according to Marius Bewley "looked like visiting royalty," was closely associated with the gallery, as a friend of Peggy's, an art collector, and a visual artist who showed her work there. Her presence brought Art of This Century a sexy cachet and attracted an audience who might otherwise have been less interested in modern art.

Peggy was thrilled by the gallery's popularity, and though Max enjoyed the opening ("He was a cross between the prince regent and the museum's biggest star"), her happiness at work underlined her misery at Hale House. "All this was exciting and new, and I was delighted to get away from home, where I always felt Max did not love me." She feared she was alienating him further "with my endless talking about the museum, how many people came and how many catalogues I had sold."

There was plenty for Peggy to talk about: the artists who began using the gallery as an informal meeting place and the art students to whom the place became a pilgrimage spot. "It was our high school," recalls the painter Paul Resika. The gallery was used as a background for fashion shoots in *Vogue* and *Glamour* and was the subject of a photo feature in the *New York Times Magazine*. It was often crowded, and though Peggy tried to stay in her office, she was too excited and kept rushing out to ask people what they thought of the installation and the art.

As frequently happened when Peggy felt that her spending was veering out of control, or that people were taking advantage of her, she became obsessed with small sums. For a while she insisted on charging an admission fee of twenty-five cents, a policy she strictly enforced; when Jimmy Ernst allowed his friends to enter without paying, Peggy waited downstairs in the lobby, counting the number of people who rode up in the elevator and correlating the total against the contents of the tambourine that collected coins. Eventually, Howard Putzel persuaded her that admission should be free.

Though it was the most spare and the least theatrical of the exhibition spaces, the Daylight Gallery, with its temporary shows, had the greatest impact on American art, for it was there that a new generation of artists found encouragement and recognition. Meanwhile Peggy's collection expanded as she purchased works from the Daylight Gallery.

The first of the fifty-five shows that were held there featured a display of Surrealist objects: another edition (one was on permanent display in the Kinetic gallery) of the little "valise" that Marcel Duchamp had assembled from a Louis Vuitton suitcase and the materials he'd sent from Europe along with Peggy's household goods; boxes made by Joseph Cornell; and wine bottles painted and decorated by Laurence Vail.

In the spring of 1943, the Daylight Gallery hosted the first exhibition of collages in the United States; the show included pieces by established artists—Arp, Picasso, Braque, Schwitters —and by emerging talents including Ad Reinhardt, Robert Motherwell, and Jackson Pollock. Having been told by James Johnson Sweeney that Pollock was doing interesting work, Peggy encouraged Pollock to submit work for the collage exhibition.

Pollock had never worked in collage before, nor did he much want to do so, but an invitation to show at Art of This Century was irresistible. He and Motherwell worked together, producing collages that Motherwell found inspiring and useful, but which failed to interest Pollock, the viewers, or the critics, and which he eventually destroyed.

Pollock's first solo show, in November 1943, was followed by one of "Natural, Insane, and Surrealist Art," which brought together skeletons, driftwood, tree roots, works done by inmates of European asylums, and drawings, watercolors, and small sculptures by Calder, Cornell, Klee, Masson, Motherwell, and Pollock. There were shows of Hans Hofmann, de Chirico, and (in January 1945) Mark Rothko, whom Peggy had been reluctant to take on until Howard Putzel invited her to his own apartment, where, to make his point, he had hung a Rothko painting on every wall.

In the autumn of 1944, a concert was held at Art of This Century to mark the release of the gallery's first foray into the production of musical recordings. With a cover designed by Max Ernst—a reproduction of the cover of the *Art of This Century* catalogue—the album contained three 78 rpm records of music by Paul Bowles; his *Sonata for Flute and Piano* occupied five sides of the records, and the sixth contained his *Two Mexican Dances*. Introduced by the composer Virgil Thomson, with whom Bowles had worked at the *New York Herald Tribune*, Peggy, Paul Bowles, and his wife, the hugely original novelist and playwright Jane Bowles, had become friends. There was some hope that this would lead to other musical productions under the gallery's aegis, but the Bowles record remained the only one.

Among the most remarkable aspects of Art of This Century was the unusual amount of attention paid to women artists. During the time that the gallery was in operation there were two major group shows and a dozen solo shows of work by women; even more extraordinary for that time (as indeed it would be now), almost forty percent of the art on view over the life of the Daylight Gallery was made by women.

Equally striking is how few of these women—Frida Kahlo, Louise Bourgeois, and Leonora Carrington—went on to develop careers and reputations remotely approaching those of their male contemporaries. Most of them—Alice Trumbull Mason, Dolia Loriant, Pamela Bodin, Teresa Zarnower, Sonja Sekula, and many others—are now largely unknown.

The first of these group shows was entitled "Exhibition by 31 Women." A jury composed of Peggy, Breton, Duchamp, Max and Jimmy Ernst, James Thrall Soby, and James Johnson Sweeney was convened to choose the artists.

One can only speculate about the reasons why Peggy would have suggested that her notoriously unfaithful husband be the one to visit the studios of the women candidates and make the final selections. Later Max would joke that he had slept with all thirty-one of the women except for Gypsy Rose Lee, who wasn't at home . . . but her maid was.

Perhaps on some level Peggy wanted Max to meet a woman who might end their failing marriage, for that was precisely what happened. When Max visited the studio of the young and beautiful Dorothea Tanning, they fell in love.

Tanning's book *Birthday*, an account of her life with Ernst, could hardly be less like Peggy's memoir: its tone is arty, poetic, wildly romantic, and more or less humorless. Reading it, one can understand why Tanning so irked Peggy, who is mentioned only as "the gentle collector of painting" who rescued Max from Europe and brought him to the United States. Tanning's account of the beginning of her love affair with Max fails to note that he was married to the gentle collector.

Tanning describes Ernst, vetting the art to be shown in the "31 Women" show, arriving at her studio on a snowy winter day. Studying a self-portrait, he asked what it was called, and when she answered she hadn't yet thought of a title, he replied—"just like that"—that she should call it *Birthday*, an idea whose brilliance she recognized at once. Noticing a photo of a chessboard, he asked whether she played chess, and they played in total silence until it grew dark and stopped snowing. Tanning lost the match.

On the following day Max returned to play more chess and offered to give Dorothea some pointers. "So the next day and the next saw us playing frantic chess. Calycine layers of an old husk, decorum, kept me sitting in the prim chair instead of starred on the bed. Until a week went by and he came to stay."

> It took only a few hours for him to move in. There was no discussion. It was as if he had found a house. Yes, I think I was his house. He lived in me; he decorated me; he watched over me. . . . It was above all so natural and right, I thought; the long wait on the station platform was rewarded by the arrival of the train, as one knew it would be, sooner or later.

Back at Hale House, Peggy was growing more desperately unhappy. For if it had been her intention to replace herself, to find Max a new lover, one would never know it from her often-repeated quip that she should have limited the show to thirty women, or from her memoir, which devotes its more venomous passages to the rival who, in the first edition, Peggy calls Annacia Tinning and whom she describes as "pretentious, boring, stupid, vulgar, and dressed in the worst possible taste but [who] was quite talented and imitated Max's painting, which flattered him immensely."

The early months of 1943 were especially trying ones for Peggy. Max left her for Dorothea. The John Cage concert that she had hoped to stage at her gallery instead took place at the Museum of Modern Art. Jimmy Ernst quit Art of This Century to help his girlfriend Elenor open the Norlyst Gallery. And Hale House was sold, requiring Peggy to find a new home, a change she claimed to welcome, since the Beekman Place apartment had become a depressing reminder of her life there with Max.

But by spring, things had begun to improve. Peggy hired Howard Putzel to direct the gallery. The jury assembled to select works for the "Spring Salon for Young Artists" chose a canvas by Jackson Pollock, who—having been fired from his WPA job painting canvases for government office buildings and having been reduced to shoplifting art supplies—was working as a handyman, elevator operator, and framer at the Museum of Non-Objective Painting, under the bullying leadership of the Baroness Hilla Rebay.

Stenographic Figure, the ambitious work that Pollock had submitted, was five and a half feet long. It had impressed the jury, but as would happen later with Mark Rothko, Peggy had to be convinced, and this time Piet Mondrian took on the job of persuading her.

Jimmy Ernst recalls, "Peggy joined Mondrian, who stood rooted in front of the Pollocks. 'Pretty awful, isn't it? That's not painting, is it?' When Mondrian did not respond, she walked away. Twenty minutes later he was still studying the same paintings, his right hand thoughtfully stroking his chin. Peggy talked to him again. 'There is absolutely no discipline at all. This young man has serious problems . . . and painting is one of them . . .'"

> Mondrian continued to stare at the Pollocks, but then turned to her. "Peggy, I don't know. I have a feeling that this may be the most exciting painting that I have seen in a long time, here or in Europe."

Peggy was further encouraged by the opinions of artists she respected, by James Johnson Sweeney, whom she had begun to rely on as she'd once depended on Herbert Read, and, after the show opened, by the response of the press. Among the favorable notices was Robert Coates's, in the *New Yorker*, which called Pollock "a real discovery." A piece in *The Nation* by Peggy's friend Jean Connolly noted that Pollock's painting had left the jury "starry-eyed."

Peggy's enthusiasm for Pollock grew, and she began to consider giving him a solo show. When Peggy told Sweeney that she was concerned because Pollock's work seemed wild and difficult to categorize, he replied that those were exactly the reasons to show it; in her memoir Peggy refers to Pollock as the "spiritual offspring" to whom she and Sweeney had given birth.

Her June 1943 visit to Pollock's studio on East 8th Street was a near disaster. Pollock and his future wife, the painter Lee Krasner, had been to a friend's wedding at which Pollock—the best man—had gotten drunk and passed out. By the time they'd hurried back to 8th Street, where they'd left the door open because they were afraid of being late, they found Peggy leaving the building, furious at having been kept waiting. Her irritation grew when she saw that many of the paintings had been done by Krasner, in whom—as Peggy instantly announced—she had no interest. Krasner would never forgive her.

From then on the two women had a contentious relationship, their disagreements tempered by their shared faith in, and devotion to, Pollock. In 1961, the artist's widow and his former dealer were to become involved in an expensive and acrimonious lawsuit motivated by the dramatic spike in the price of his paintings, and by Peggy's belief that Pollock and Krasner had cheated her—by hiding and withholding paintings—according to the terms of his contracts with Art of This Century.

Peggy offered Pollock the first of those contracts not long after that initial studio visit, in the spring of 1943. She also agreed to give Pollock a one-man show the following November. To enable him to complete enough paintings to fill the Daylight Gallery, she would pay him $150 a month, an advance which (minus her dealer's fee) would be deducted from his sales; if he didn't sell a sufficient amount of work to repay Peggy's investment, she could recover the balance in paintings.

This agreement enabled Pollock to quit his menial job at the Museum of Non-Objective Painting. Peggy was thrilled to be able to rescue a talented young artist from the clutches of the Baroness Rebay, to take some small revenge for having been accused of capitalizing on the Guggenheim name in her vulgar efforts to peddle art. Peggy had continued to despise Rebay, who had made no secret of her disdain for Pollock. At a ritual viewing of her employees' work, she had ripped up one of his drawings.

Though such arrangements are more common today, it was the first time that Pollock or anyone in his circle had heard of a modern artist being offered this sort of patronage. Pollock was delighted, and Peggy was likewise happy to begin an association with a painter whom she would later call her most important discovery.

Though Peggy had sexual relationships with a number of artists whose work she showed, this was not the case with Pollock. The brooding, hulking, barely verbal painter seems not to have appealed to Peggy, who had always been attracted to conventionally handsome men, articulate conversationalists who made a point of knowing more than she did. It is also possible that Peggy, having just endured the prolonged, theatrical, and wounding end of her marriage to Max Ernst, was tired and taking a break, of sorts, from Eros.

Around this time, Peggy grew close to Kenneth Macpherson, a homosexual Scottish art collector to whom she would develop a strong, unclear, and ultimately unsatisfying attachment. They decided to live together, and Peggy found a suitable apartment on East 61st Street. The duplex would not be ready until the fall, and they agreed to spend the summer in Connecticut, near where Laurence Vail and Jean Connolly were vacationing, on the shore of Candlewood Lake, "where Jews were not supposed to bathe." Clearly, certain things hadn't changed all that much since Peggy and her relatives had been turned away from the posh and restrictive hotels.

Unable to persuade Macpherson to sign the lease, Peggy sent Paul Bowles to negotiate the rental agreement. "The house was horrid, but the non-Jewish lake was nice and just in front of our door." She enjoyed her domestic life with Macpherson, "an excellent cook and a very particular housekeeper. . . . I lived with Kenneth during those three weeks in every respect but one. I never slept with him. One night he said I should share his bed because I was so frightened. We had come across a corpse or a crouching figure of some kind in Jean's garden. It was after a party and we were walking home. By the time we went back to fetch a light the corpse had disappeared, but not its terrifying memory."

That autumn, Peggy and Macpherson moved into the duplex, where their relationship was further complicated by the bizarre architecture of their apartment, which had been created by combining two living spaces on different levels with minimal regard for the comfort and privacy of its inhabitants and with the kitchen and the bathrooms in inconvenient places. Initially, Peggy referred to Macpherson as her lover. She liked the attention he paid her and welcomed his interest in helping her become a more chic and stylish version of her younger self. In the first version of her memoir, the chapter about their life together is entitled "Peace."

> At this time Kenneth and I were very happy together. He depended on me and would have been quite lost without me. If he ever felt he was losing me, he turned on all his charm to get me back. . . . I really think that at this time Kenneth half considered me his wife.

Half considered? Rather less than *half*, as it would turn out. Other passages in the memoir may alert readers to the fragility of Peggy and Kenneth's bliss. "Because of Kenneth's very strong influence over me, I suddenly completely changed my style of dress. I tried to stop looking like a slut and bought some expensive clothes. . . . He hated red so much that though it was my favorite color I entirely gave up wearing anything that approached it. I bought a little blue suit with buttons, which he adored, because he said I looked like a little boy in it. He loved what he called my gamin quality."

Jean Connolly, who had been married to the British poet Cyril Connolly and who would soon marry Laurence Vail, not only moved in with Peggy but slept in the same bed, which disturbed Kenneth. "Even though he must have known that our relationship was perfectly innocent, I felt he objected to her being there."

Peggy's memoirs are never more lurid or excessively confessional than when she is describing the breakup of a marriage or romance, and such is the case with her account of how badly things went wrong with Macpherson. One night, Peggy wanted to stay in Kenneth's bed, and Kenneth asked: How could Peggy even *think* about such a thing when David was coming tomorrow. David?

Peggy had visited David Larkins—Kenneth's lover—on a trip to see Sindbad, who was stationed at the same military base in Tampa. Larkins had been in traction, in an army hospital, recovering from an accident.

> I told [Larkins], in the most garrulous way, all about the duplex and our summer plans, never dreaming how he was to be the instrument of evil and destruction in my life. . . .
> Unfortunately, he too was secretly in love with Kenneth.
> . . . Later I wrote to him from Connecticut, never dreaming what harm he was about to do me.

Soon after his arrival in New York, Larkins became a constant presence in the duplex, and a source of conflict between Kenneth and Peggy. At the end of one particularly dreadful evening, David attempted to seduce Peggy, but a few nights later he informed her that he couldn't feel any real desire for a woman because he preferred choirboys.

As the truth about Macpherson's sexuality became increasingly difficult to ignore, Peggy was obliged to modify her illusions about their future together. Kenneth instructed Peggy never to use the word *homosexual* or its slang equivalents, and to speak of him and his lovers as "Athenian," a term Peggy would continue to use among the many Athenian friends she would later make in Venice. Meanwhile a rebellious and increasingly frustrated Peggy began referring to Kenneth as her "lesbian friend." One night, in front of his friends, Macpherson said that Peggy had made him sign the lease so she wouldn't be responsible. He announced that he hated his life in the apartment and wished he'd never moved there. Peggy and Kenneth had planned to throw a housewarming party together, but now Kenneth told her that he wanted to give his own celebration. Her name wouldn't even appear on the invitation.

One night, at midnight, Peggy's doorbell rang. Pegeen had come "home from Mexico at last. She wore a raincoat and carried a little bag, having lost everything else at the frontier. She looked like such a baby, it really was pathetic. We showed her the duplex, which she had so much encouraged us to take in the spring, and the room which I had built for her. She was glad to be home but quite lost in this new setting. Complications arose at once. She was jealous of Kenneth and he was jealous of her." Peggy describes her daughter following her when she went upstairs to be with Kenneth. It was, Peggy decided, "quite natural as I provided no home life for her downstairs, being perpetually with Kenneth in his flat at this time. When she followed me upstairs, I invited her into Kenneth's flat, and he was annoyed that I should take such liberties."

Having disliked high school and refused to go to college, Pegeen had left Manhattan for Mexico. During a stay on a yacht belonging to Errol Flynn, whose relationships with underage girls had gotten him into trouble with the law, she had contracted a venereal disease. Subsequently, she had fallen in love with a Mexican diver named Chango, and had been living with him and his family in Acapulco. Her situation was so unstable and her mental and physical health so frail that Leonora

Carrington, now living in Mexico, became concerned, and Laurence Vail had been delegated to go to Acapulco and bring Pegeen home.

Having belonged to several households that imploded when her parents found other mates, having seen her mother take up with a succession of unsuitable men and her father abandoned by her stepmother, having been tossed by the storms of Peggy's relationship with Max Ernst, Pegeen had grown into a shy, damaged, and insecure young woman, subject to spells of sadness and self-loathing. It was her misfortune, or one of her misfortunes, to have gotten into such serious trouble just when her mother was negotiating her doomed relationship with Kenneth Macpherson and was also extremely busy at the gallery; indeed, it was the most important and exciting moment in Peggy's professional life.

Peggy was grateful to Laurence, as she frequently was, for having stepped in and taken responsibility for their daughter. Although Pegeen was often depressed, Peggy chose to assume that if her daughter moved back in with her, worked on her art, and learned to coexist with Kenneth, Pegeen's problems would vanish and she would stop announcing that she wanted to return to Acapulco and marry Chango.

In December 1944 Pegeen secretly married Jean Hélion, the dashing Frenchman whose abstract canvases Peggy had shown soon after Art of This Century opened. His show's popularity owed partly to the public lecture in which Hélion recounted his escape from a German prisoner-of-war camp and his journey across war-ravaged Europe. At the time of their marriage, Pegeen was nineteen and Hélion was forty. The couple soon moved to France, where they would have three sons (the couple had two, and Hélion adopted the son whom Pegeen had with another man) before divorcing in 1958.

Pollock

> Pollock immediately became the central point
> of Art of This Century. From . . . 1943, until I left
> America in 1947, I dedicated myself to Pollock.

PEGGY UNDERSTOOD that she was taking a risk in devoting so much money, time, and energy to furthering Jackson Pollock's career. His abstractions continued to disquiet many of the art buyers who frequented Art of This Century, and his rough, uncompromising personality did little to reassure, amuse, or beguile them. He was temperamentally incapable of socializing with potential collectors and patrons—a talent that was as important then as it is for artists today.

Charming the rich came naturally to Robert Motherwell, who had been educated at Harvard. But it posed more of a challenge for the shy, alcoholic Pollock, who, when he drank, could become "unpleasant, one might say devilish. . . . He was like a trapped animal who should never have left Wyoming, where he was born." Nonetheless, Peggy was confident and optimistic enough to write to Grace McCann Morley, director of the San Francisco Museum of Art, saying that she hoped to send a traveling show of Pollock's work cross-country. And Peggy took an ad in *Art Digest* in which she called Pollock "one of the strongest and most interesting American painters."

Peggy commissioned James Johnson Sweeney to write the copy for the exhibition catalogue that accompanied Pollock's first solo show. The curator called Pollock's talent "volcanic . . . lavish . . . explosive," and described the artist as brave in his determination to go his own way without worrying about how his work would be received by the public. "It spills out in a mineral prodigality not yet crystallized."

The opening on November 9 was sparsely attended; among the few guests was Joseph Cornell. Pollock got so drunk that, in order to get him downstairs, someone had to put him in a chair and load it into the elevator.

The show received more attention from the press than any previous Art of This Century exhibition. Robert Coates, writing in the *New Yorker*, reiterated his conviction that Pollock was something genuinely new, and in *The Nation*, Clement Greenberg, who was to be one of Pollock's most passionate supporters, wrote that the smaller canvases in particular were among "the strongest abstract works I have yet seen by an American." To Robert Motherwell, Pollock represented "one of the younger generation's chances. There are not three other painters of whom this could be said."

None of the paintings sold, though three drawings were bought by friends of Peggy's, among them Kenneth Macpherson, who had helped hang the show.

Thirty years after the first version of her memoir was published, Peggy expanded on it, adding a section about the installation of Pollock's mural in the hall of the 61st Street apartment. Commissioning the mural represented the spectacular coup of having the most important young painter decorate your corridor, and in the process setting something free in the painter himself; in part this may have been a positive effect of the physical scale—the sheer size—of the work he'd been engaged to do. Peggy tells the dramatic (if apocryphal) story about Pollock being blocked and then painting the whole mural in three hours. She describes the difficult installation: the painting was too big for the site, and at the last minute the problem was solved by Duchamp and a workman. And she includes its aftermath: Pollock got so drunk that he walked naked into a party that Jean Connolly was giving. An equally well-known and possibly mythical (surely Peggy would have told it, were it true) version is that Pollock walked through the living room and urinated into the fireplace.

For Peggy, the punch line was neither Pollock's artistic breakthrough nor his bad behavior but rather the fact that this important work of modern art irritated Kenneth. "I liked the mural but Kenneth couldn't bear it. He never allowed me to light it, saying the light I had specially installed for it blew out all the fuses, so it could only be seen in the daytime or when I went down and put the lights on surreptitiously." In a letter to Emily Coleman, Peggy wrote about the mural, "Everyone likes it except Kenneth. Rather bad luck on him as he has to see it every time he goes in or out."

Not long after Pollock's first Art of This Century show, the Museum of Modern Art bought a painting, *The She-Wolf*, for six hundred dollars; it had put a reserve on the work before the exhibition began. And over the next few years, quite a few of Pollock's works would make their way into private and museum collections.

Despite the lackluster sales from the first show, Peggy (with the encouragement of James Johnson Sweeney and the painter Hans Hofmann) extended Pollock's contract for another year, and Pollock's second Art of This Century show opened, for a monthlong run, beginning on March 19, 1945. This time Pollock worked at a greatly accelerated pace; even so, the show was initially postponed because not enough paintings had been completed. The opening was better attended than the party that had inaugurated the earlier exhibition, and many guests took advantage of the invitation (extended in the catalogue) to view the mural in Peggy's corridor, which was open to the public for three hours on the afternoon of the opening.

The show featured thirteen paintings, as well as drawings and gouaches. The British collector Dwight Ripley and the San Francisco Museum of Art each acquired a painting, and during the following year, other paintings went to the Norton Museum in Palm Beach, Florida, and the National Gallery of Australia in Canberra. Under the terms of her contract, Peggy got two paintings, one of which she donated to the University of Iowa in 1947; the other, entitled *Two*, remained in her collection. Once more there was a heartening response from the press, much of it positive, though the *New York Times* critic observed that Pollock's work resembled "an explosion in a shingle mill."

That fall, Pollock and Lee Krasner got married. Peggy was unenthusiastic about the upcoming nuptials. "Why are you getting married? You're married enough," was the understandable, if somewhat disingenuous, reaction of a woman who had been married twice. Claiming that she had to go to lunch with a collector, Peggy skipped the wedding.

Hoping that Pollock's drinking and depression might improve, and that he might find it easier to work if they lived in the country, Krasner persuaded him to move to a house they found in Springs, on Long Island, near East Hampton. Lacking the two thousand dollars they needed for a down payment, Krasner approached Peggy, who was sick with the flu. Peggy replied that she was a dealer, not a bank, and told Krasner to get a job—or else ask rival dealer Sam Kootz for the money.

When Krasner took Peggy at her word, and Kootz agreed—provided that Pollock come over to his gallery—Peggy was outraged, but Krasner's approach succeeded in persuading her to come up with the two thousand dollars and to double Pollock's monthly stipend.

March 1946 was an eventful month for Peggy. The first edition of *Out of This Century* appeared and was advertised in *View* magazine as "the revealing picture of a woman who never learned to live cautiously"—a lack of caution that presumably carried over into the scandalous content of her memoir. Peggy spent much of that spring dealing with the repercussions. Among the problems she faced was her publisher's mistake in attributing the design of her gallery, in a photo caption, to Berenice Abbott, who had simply taken the picture. Fredrick Kiesler insisted that a correction slip be included in each copy of the book, and in a radio interview on WNYC, Peggy made a point of addressing this error.

Preoccupied by the hoopla surrounding her book, Peggy had limited energy for the show of Pegeen's work; the exhibition coincided with the appearance of *Out of This Century*, which not only included scathing portraits of Pegeen's father and stepmother but also intimate revelations about her mother's abortions and sexual history. At Pegeen's first solo show—she had previously been included in group shows of women artists—she sold two paintings and two gouaches. Reviews praised the primitive sophistication—or was it the sophisticated primitivism? —of her work, which received more favorable notice than the "biomorphic abstractions" of Pollock's friend Peter Busa, whose paintings were displayed at the same time as Pegeen's.

At the end of March, Pegeen's work came down from the walls of the Daylight Gallery and Jackson Pollock's went up. Soon after, Pegeen moved to Paris with Jean Hélion.

Pollock's third solo show, which opened on April 2, consisted of eleven oil paintings and eight temperas, most of which

Pollock had done before he and Krasner moved to Springs. His work continued to sell; eleven pieces were purchased that year. Still, the money that came in failed to pay off Peggy's advance, and, according to the terms of their contract, she acquired so many of his paintings that she gave quite a few of them away before she moved back to Europe. Later she would deeply regret these acts of generosity.

A collector of European art, Lydia Winston Malbin, offers a glimpse of Peggy at work as she recalls the zeal with which Peggy persuaded her to acquire a Pollock instead of the Masson she had come into the gallery to buy:

> Peggy was at her desk and I asked her if she had any drawings by Masson. . . . We talked a little and Peggy asked me if I had ever heard of Jackson Pollock. This was, as far as I can remember, a new name to me, and I was impressed with Peggy's sincerity and enthusiasm. We went back to her storage room, and she brought out some of Pollock's canvases. I was immediately interested in them. There was a kind of formless, elusive structure, a web of black and rich colors. . . . I thought about this and then went back to Peggy's gallery. I acquired Pollock's 1945 "Moon Vessel" for $275 and took it home on the train. Some of my friends criticized it so much I didn't hang it with the rest of my collection right away.

Though none of the critics could summon quite the same enthusiasm they'd shown for previous shows, the fact of Pollock's talent was established.

By that summer, Peggy had begun thinking about moving back to Europe. Pegeen was with Jean Hélion in Paris, where Sindbad was working as an army interpreter. Laurence Vail had married Jean Connolly and departed for France to reclaim his houses in Megève and his father's Paris apartment. In June, Peggy went to England in the hopes of locating some possessions she had lost when she'd left London before the war. In Paris she met her friend Mary McCarthy and her husband,

Bowden Broadwater, who persuaded her to accompany them to Venice.

Peggy had met McCarthy on Cape Cod, when she and Max had summered there in 1942; that year, McCarthy's book *The Company She Keeps* had brought her recognition and (thanks to its frank portrait of a modern and independent young woman) notoriety. Though their backgrounds were very different— McCarthy was an Irish Catholic from Seattle whose parents had died in the 1918 influenza epidemic and who had been raised by relatives—they shared a waspish sense of humor, an interest in literature and art, and a fierce determination to live without worrying about society's opinion. Both took lovers when they wished, exchanged one man for another, and became romantically involved with men whose sexuality was ambiguous.

Peggy traveled with McCarthy and Broadwater to Venice by train, an arduous journey interrupted in Lausanne when McCarthy became too ill to go on and had to recuperate in a Swiss hospital. The three were reunited in Venice, which would become the setting for McCarthy's short story "The Cicerone," notable for its literary portrait of Peggy, thinly disguised as an American traveler named Polly Herkimer Grabbe.

McCarthy's portrayal of Polly, a flower-bulb heiress, reduces its real-life model's collection of modern art to a collection of garden statuary, changes her career to that of "an impresario of modern architecture," whatever that might mean, and is dismissive of her accomplishments. "She imagined that she came abroad out of cultural impatience with America; in her own eyes, she was always a rebel against a commercial civilization. She hoped to be remembered for her architectural experiments, her patronage of the arts, her championship of personal freedom, and flattered herself that in Europe this side of her was taken seriously." The familiar charges of parsimony (or of an unseemly interest in money) are leveled against Polly Grabbe. "Miss Grabbe's intelligence was flighty . . . but her

estimates were sharp; no contractor or husband had ever pad-
ded a bill on her; she always put on her glasses to add up a dinner check." And McCarthy is contemptuous of Polly/Peggy's
wealth: "Having money, she had little real curiosity; she was
not a dependent of the world. . . . She was not, despite appearances, a woman of strong convictions. . . . Her money had
made her insular; she was used to a mercenary circle and had no
idea that outside it lovers showed affection, friends repaid
kindness, and husbands did not ask an allowance or bring their
mistress home to bed."

The narrative's view of Peggy is, at moments, psychologically accurate: "Miss Grabbe seemed to have been parched and
baked by exposure, hardened and chapped by the winds of re-
buff and failure. . . . An indefatigable Narcissa, she adapted
herself spryly to comedy when she perceived that the world
was smiling; she was always the second to laugh at a pratfall of
her spirit." Ultimately, though, McCarthy's version of Peggy is
a sneering one. "Miss Grabbe, despite her boldness, was not an
original woman, and her boldness, in fact, consisted in taking
everything literally. She made love in Europe because it was
the thing to do."

Scattered throughout this portrait of a silly and promiscuous woman are occasional flashes of admiration, particularly
for Polly's courage and her ability to "say good-bye and to look
ahead for the next thing," which in Peggy/Polly's case means a
new life in Venice, where she has begun to talk about finding a
palazzo in which to live: "Her trip to Italy . . . had the character of a farewell and a new beginning, and [her] hotel suite . . .
resembled a branch office which had been opened but was not
yet in full operation." Unlike the American tourist couple at
the center of the story, Polly is an "explorer."

During that trip to Venice, Peggy was already contacting
artists and real estate agents, trying to figure out how she could

live there. Directed to the Café All'Angelo, where local painters and sculptors congregated, she realized that she would be
welcomed by the Venetian art world, which was sorely in need
of an infusion of energy, creativity, a broadly international out-
look, and foreign money.

In the fall, Peggy went back to New York, but this time
she knew, and let it be known, that her return was temporary. There was little in the United States to keep her. She had
grown tired of the gallery and resentful of the amount of time
and energy it demanded. In October, her divorce from Max
Ernst became official, and three days later Max and Dorothea
were married in Los Angeles. Marius Bewley left the gallery
and was replaced by Tom Dunn, and Peggy began making arrangements to donate works to private museums—to the University of Iowa, the San Francisco Museum of Art, and the Yale
University Library. Over the next dozen years, she would make
more than 150 such donations.

Never one to keep her plans a secret, Peggy stirred up
considerable unease when she returned from Europe and announced that she had come back to New York only to put her
affairs in order. Many artists had come to depend on Peggy, and
many more hoped that they would come to depend on Peggy;
their futures seemed far more uncertain when it became clear
that she would no longer be around to promote their art.

Jackson Pollock, whose earnings career had not yet enabled him to stop worrying about paying the mortgage on the
house in Springs, asked to have one last show before Art of
This Century closed. The fourth and last Art of This Century
Pollock show opened on January 14, 1947, and was supposed to
end on February 1 but was extended another week.

Included in the exhibition were fifteen major paintings,
done since Pollock and Lee Krasner had moved to Long Island; the first few had been done in an upstairs bedroom, the

later ones in the barn that he had set up as a studio, and which is where (thanks to the historic *Life* magazine photographs and Hans Namuth's films and photos) we visualize him painting. The *Accabonac Creek* paintings were bright, vaguely representational canvases, while the *Sounds in the Grass* series marked the shift to the poured swirls and drips of his best-known work.

The show was praised by Clement Greenberg, and Peggy made an effort to sell the new paintings, along with the older ones in her collection. Meanwhile, she looked for a dealer to take over her contract with Pollack. Like so much of what Peggy did, her efforts were simultaneously generous and self-serving: she made sure not only that Pollock's work continued to be shown but also that she would continue to receive revenue from the sale of his paintings. Given the rarity of such contracts and the fact that Pollock's reputation was still not entirely established, it was a challenge to persuade Betty Parsons to take on Pollock as a client and to put on a show of Pollock's work in January 1948.

After the final Pollock show at Art of This Century, there were only four more Daylight Gallery exhibitions: including one by Morris Hirshfield, a self-taught outsider artist who had made his living as a manufacturer of women's bedroom slippers; another by a young Abstract Expressionist, Richard Pousette-Dart, whose painting Peggy had added to her collection; and a third by the sculptor David Hare.

The final show was a retrospective of the work of Theo van Doesburg, the late husband of Nellie van Doesburg, with whom Peggy had escaped from Paris a few days before the German invasion. Peggy had worked hard but had failed to get Nellie admitted to the United States before the war, and Nellie had spent the war years in Europe.

For all of Peggy's desire to be unconventional and unpredictable, she enjoyed ceremony and was fond of the grand and sentimental gesture. Closing Art of This Century with a show of Theo van Doesburg's work was intended to signify that her collection had come full circle, from Europe to America and back again to Europe. It was an act of friendship and loyalty honoring those early years in Paris and celebrating everything that had happened in between.

The final show received a great deal of press attention. Except for a negative review from Robert Coates in the *New Yorker*, the notices struck a tone that combined praise of van Doesburg with a valedictory for Peggy, and acclaim for the remarkable achievements of Art of This Century.

Venice

AT PRECISELY the right moment, Peggy's accountant, Bernard Reis, managed to perform the inheritance-law version of a magic trick: he'd figured out how to break one of Peggy's trusts and free up enough money so that—despite the expenses of having lived lavishly for years in New York, despite the cost of continuing to acquire art, despite the fact that the gallery had failed to make a profit—Peggy could contemplate buying a palazzo in Venice. This turned out to be more difficult than renting luxury apartments on the East Side of Manhattan, and while Peggy endeavored (with the help of Pegeen) to find the right place, she rented a floor of the Palazzo Barbaro, in which Henry James had written *The Aspern Papers* and set a scene in *The Wings of the Dove.*

That November she escaped the winter cold and traveled to Capri. Now married to Jean Connolly, Laurence Vail had made a sentimental return to the island that he and Peggy had visited at the start of their married life and where they had been joined by Laurence's sister Clothilde, whose disruptive presence had caused Peggy such pain. Peggy rented the Villa Esmeralda and found herself at the center of a lively social scene that included Kenneth Macpherson, who had his own Capri villa. That summer was a wild one, involving heavy drinking, complicated love affairs, rapidly changing partners, and sexual experimentation.

In the midst of it, Peggy received an invitation: thanks in part to Giuseppe Santomaso, one of the artists she'd met in Venice, she was asked to show her collection at the Twenty-Fourth Venice Biennale, which would take place the following spring. This was not only an honor but an excellent deal, because the Biennale was willing to pay the costs of shipping the collection from New York to Venice. Peggy had always delighted in being courted, perhaps because she had been obliged to do so much of the seduction herself. Now she was being wooed by Venice, by government officials and artists who understood how much her presence would benefit the city.

Begun in the late nineteenth century and still highly influential today, the Venice Biennale brings prominent artists, critics, dealers, and collectors to exhibit and view art in a cluster of pavilions located in the Arsenale district; each pavilion represents a foreign country and showcases that nation's artists. The range of Peggy's collection would provide a broader and less strictly nationalistic sense of what had mattered in art for the previous thirty years and what was happening at the current moment, in Europe and in the United States.

The Greek pavilion that Peggy was assigned had fallen into disrepair, and the gifted Venetian architect Carlo Scarpa was engaged to remodel it. Her exhibition opened at the start of the Bienniale, on June 6, and was a great success. It was much talked about by European visitors, many of whom had never seen the work of the Abstract Expressionists and who were limited in their knowledge of modern art. Peggy was pleased by the result; in her memoir, she writes that seeing her name surrounded by the names of so many foreign nations made her feel as if she were "a new European country." And she proudly toured the pavilion with the visitors who passed through Venice that summer—among them, Alfred Barr, Marc Chagall, Matta, the Reises, and Roland Penrose and his wife, Lee Miller.

After the Biennale, Peggy's collection traveled to Florence and Milan, and later to Amsterdam, Brussels, and Zurich while she negotiated with the Italian government about how much duty she would have to pay in order to move her paintings and sculpture permanently to Italy. After the Zurich show, the art was officially classified as being imported from Switzerland and was consequently taxed at a lower rate. Peggy and her collection were reunited in Venice in 1951.

By then, she had bought and was living in the Palazzo Venier dei Leoni. Construction on the palace had started in the eighteenth century, but had been interrupted, and the one-story structure facing the Grand Canal in the Dorsoduro district was known thereafter as the unfinished palace. Because the palazzo had, in theory, remained a work in progress, it was not subject to the same tight restrictions on rebuilding and remodeling as were other Venetian landmarks, and Peggy set about renovating her new home. When plans for a second story proved impractical, she added a pavilion, known as a *barchessa* (a word used, on farms, to denote a structure designed to store hay), in the garden, and she installed her paintings and sculptures in rooms and outdoor spaces designed to represent a cross between traditional Venetian elegance and something more spare and modern. The decoration of the palazzo was an ongoing process. In 1961, Peggy hired Claire Falkenstein to fashion the gates that can still be seen today, hand-welded from small pieces of iron and brightened by glittering shards of Murano glass.

According to Peggy, no proper Venetian approved of her modern décor or of her taste in art. "Princess Pignatelli once said to me, 'If you would only throw all those awful pictures into the Grand Canal, you would have the most beautiful house in Venice.'" But Peggy felt that the furnishings needed to complement the collection. "In place of a Venetian glass chandelier, I hung a Calder mobile, made of broken glass and china that might have come out of a garbage pail."

Peggy immediately set out to establish a salon and hosted parties and dinners to which she invited a range of guests that included Prince Philip, Tennessee Williams, Giacometti, Mary McCarthy, and Truman Capote, who spent two months at her home, writing *The Muses Are Heard*, an account of an earlier trip to the Soviet Union. Determined to keep his weight down, Capote forced Peggy to diet along with him, allowing her to eat only fish and a "light lunch of eggs." The poet Charles Wright recalls being a young student on a Fulbright Fellowship in Venice during the terrible floods of the late 1960s. As the waters rose, he was taken in and found shelter and entertainment at a lively party held in Peggy's palazzo. "Sindbad Vail," he recalls, "was pouring the drinks."

Around the same time, playwright John Guare arrived at the Guggenheim Collection just after it closed; the museum was scheduled to remain shut for the next few days and would not open again until after Guare had left Venice. Determined to see the art, he knocked loudly on the door, which was eventually opened by "a woman in a bathrobe." She showed him around the palazzo, taking her time, leisurely discussing the paintings. And when at last he asked whether she worked there, she replied, "I'm Peggy Guggenheim!" Guare was by no means the only visitor taken for a private tour by Peggy, who had resolutely and rather dramatically resisted Herbert Read's suggestion that her collection not be opened to the public.

Peggy continued to discover and encourage young Italian artists, whose work she added to her collection; among these new protégés were Edmondo Bacci and Tancredi Parmeggiani. Meanwhile, the fact that she had opened her home to the public for several days a week, so that she and her houseguests were essentially living in a museum, generated a certain confusion. John Richardson recalls that when he stayed at Peggy's palazzo, strangers frequently barged into his bedroom, imagining that it was included on the tour.

Peggy thrived on the excitement—and on her new life in Venice. She stopped dyeing her hair jet black and (aside from the elaborate and unflattering trademark butterfly sunglasses of which she was so fond and which she had specially made) she began to dress more elegantly. In pictures of her from that period, she looks prettier and certainly more stylish than she had since her youth, when she'd worn the Paul Poiret gown in which she was photographed by Man Ray.

Even as she grew older, Peggy refused to give up on the possibilities of romance, flirtation, and sex. John Richardson tells a story about staying with her in Venice, in the 1970s, when Nellie van Doesburg (who had remained a close friend) was visiting. Richardson recalls hearing the elderly friends argue about which of the hunky Italian workers restoring the palazzo each might have as her boy toy.

Peggy's last great love affair was with Raoul Gregorich, who had been born in Mestre, in the part of Venice on the mainland, and who was twenty-three years her junior. Gregorich was extremely handsome; friends of Peggy's recall him as looking like Gregory Peck. During the war he had served time in prison for an assault on the German Prince von Thurm-und-Taxis, a crime that, he convinced Peggy, had been an act of political resistance. It's notable that Peggy, whose memoir describes her marriages and romances at such length and in such intimate detail, says relatively little about Raoul, though their relationship lasted for three years.

Peggy used to tell people how happy she was that the handsome, attentive, charming Raoul had no particular interest in art or in the sort of intellectual conversations that she conducted with her friends. But the differences between them—in social class, background, age, money, and power—contributed to the turbulence of their relationship. One can hear the condescension in Sir Herbert Read's view, which Peggy quotes, that while Raoul knew nothing about art, he was "quite a philosopher." And Peggy wrote to Djuna Barnes that Raoul's sense of inferiority—a feeling with which she herself had been excruciatingly familiar—caused him to do and say terrible things.

Yet he also seems to have been capable of genuine kindness and affection. He was one of the few people who assured Peggy that she would go down in history, "which statement, though quite exaggerated, I found very touching." Others—a small and eclectic group whose members ranged from Alfred Barr to Allen Ginsberg's lover, Peter Orlovsky—were also beginning to acknowledge Peggy's historical importance.

Raoul's great passion was for motors and speed—fast boats (Peggy bought a high-powered motor boat to please him) and fast cars. The couple argued over Peggy's reluctance to give him the sports car he so desperately wanted. Finally, she gave in and bought a pale blue sports car—with tragic result. Raoul was killed driving the car she'd given him, in a crash outside Venice.

Writing to Djuna, Peggy partly blamed herself for the "Greek tragedy" of his death, for having acceded to his demands for the vehicle in which he died. But in her memoir she so distances herself from the accident that she places it between parentheses: "Raoul, who was interested only in motor cars (in one of which he was so soon after to meet his untimely death) never took much interest in art."

She writes obliquely and again almost offhandedly about her grief, yet still manages to convey how acutely she felt her lover's loss. "In the fall of 1954, after Raoul's death, I decided to get out of Italy and try to think of something else." It is typical of Peggy's literary persona that this reference to mourning so persistent that it could be escaped only by a change of scene appears as a brief introduction to a chapter about travel.

Her first stop was Ceylon, now Sri Lanka. Paul and Jane Bowles lived there, on the island that he had bought, which lacked running water and electricity, and which could be reached only by wading through the Indian Ocean. The island was only a short distance from shore, but the water was deep enough that Peggy had to pick up her skirts—and the waves still wet her bottom.

Philip Rylands, the current director of the Peggy Guggenheim Collection, remembers Peggy as having been intensely interested in other people, curious about their motives and responses. After her parties, Peggy used to ask him and his wife, Jane, who was Peggy's close friend, why this or that person had said or done whatever they had said or done.

That Peggy was so fascinated by the sources and nuances of human behavior makes it doubly striking that so little of her memoir traffics in gossip about the private lives of her friends, or about situations in which she was not directly involved. Peggy's account of her time with the Bowleses in Ceylon focuses on her visit to the home of a twelve-year-old art prodigy and a brilliant teenage cellist. She omits the fact that Paul and Jane were going through one of the crises in their marriage. Each had become deeply involved with a lover of the same sex, in Morocco. Paul had brought along his beloved Ahmed, but Jane had had no choice but to leave Cherifa (with whom she was obsessed and whom Paul's lover accused of practicing witchcraft) in her stall in the market in Tangiers. Nor did Peggy seem aware, or note in her book, that her presence precipitated a knife fight between Ahmed and the Bowleses's driver, each of whom accused the other of trying to get close to Peggy—and her money.

Jane hated Ceylon, the discomfort and the inconvenience,

and was, Peggy observed, having a nervous breakdown exacerbated by tension with Paul, by Ahmed's presence, by her inability to write, by the excitement Paul felt because he was beginning a novel, and by the impressive quantity of gin she was drinking, accompanied by a blood pressure medication and a sedative known to cause depression. After trying to persuade Jane to go to India with her, Peggy spent a week with her in Colombo.

Peggy reports only that after five weeks in Ceylon she proceeded alone to India, where, in Calcutta, she met a painter named Jaminy Roy, whose work had "a primitive quality" and who she felt was a "wise man and quite unspoilt." Peggy was unimpressed by Chandigarh, the city designed by Le Corbusier, and by modern Indian art in general, but she did like the earrings she bought in Darjeeling, where she went on an unsuccessful mission to find some Lhasa terriers so she could stop "the inbreeding of my numerous dog family."

After returning from Asia, Peggy resumed her life at the palazzo: enjoying her collection, sunbathing on the roof, touring the canals in her private gondola, entertaining visiting friends, and socializing with the transient and semipermanent coterie of homosexual men who continued to provide her with the male attention that she had always required. In addition to Truman Capote, who (with the cruelty that pervades his novel *Answered Prayers*) described a character based on Peggy as a "long-haired Bert Lahr," the men who surrounded Peggy included her old friend Charles Henri Ford, the Surrealist painter Pavel Tchelitchew, the photographer Roloff Beny, the pianists Arthur Gold and Bobby Fizdale, and the painter Robert Brady. Among the most important to Peggy was John Hohnsbeen, a former dancer and lover of the architect Philip Johnson.

Like Kenneth Macpherson, Hohnsbeen led an active social life and lived in a purely white apartment. For years, Hohnsbeen was Peggy's guest, secretary-assistant, companion, and comforter. He fully expected to be made director of the collection after Peggy's death and was angry and disappointed when the job went to Philip Rylands.

During the early 1950s, the Palazzo Venier dei Leoni became a sort of pilgrimage site/tourist destination for Beat poets and writers, whom Peggy met through the poet and playwright Alan Ansen. Ansen had been W. H. Auden's secretary, had spent time with Paul Bowles in Tangiers, and served as the model for characters in the work of Jack Kerouac and William Burroughs.

The Beat writers' visits did not always go well. Advised to kiss Peggy's hand, William Burroughs is reported to have said, "I will gladly kiss her cunt if that is the custom," a remark for which he was banned from the palazzo. Allen Ginsberg also managed to offend Peggy. At a poetry reading, Peter Orlovksy threw a sweaty towel at Ginsberg and hit Peggy by mistake. Furious, Peggy rescinded Ginsberg's invitation to a reception at her palazzo, inspiring the poet to write an abjectly apologetic letter in which he expressed eagerness to attend the party and reluctance to leave Venice without having experienced, for the first time, "a great formal historic salon" and having enjoyed "big high class social encounters." Neither man is mentioned in the final edition of *Out of This Century*.

Gregory Corso's experience with Peggy was quite different. During his lengthy stay in Venice, in 1958, he and Peggy had a quasi-romance. Like Gregorich, Corso had spent time in jail, and the poet—lean, restless, handsome, and articulate in the ways that Peggy had always found attractive—must have seemed like a revenant: the living ghost of so many of the men she had loved.

Of all the literary portraits of Peggy—in her biographies, in other writers' memoirs, as a fictional character, and in her own autobiography—Corso's is perhaps the most tender, unjudgmental, compassionate, and clear-sighted, the most resistant to the temptations of gossip and condescension.

The story of their relationship unfolds in a series of letters that Corso sent Ginsberg, beginning in January 1958, when Peggy was almost sixty and Corso was twenty-three. These letters track the beginning, the height, and the precipitous ending of the poet's romantic friendship with Peggy—and its eventual transformation into something less highly charged and more companionable.

Ginsberg seems to have told the charismatic Corso that he was capable of conning Peggy out of a lifetime's supply of dollars, to which Corso (who did indeed possess some of the talents and flaws of the con man) replied that he didn't care about money, that he needed only enough to live on and to be happy—as he already was, in Venice. He and Peggy met over dinner and drinks, and she invited him to see her collection. What happened next is worth quoting in its entirety, since—perhaps more than anything else that has been written—this evocative and rather heartbreaking passage conveys what it must have been like for a young man to find himself the object of Peggy's erotic interest:

> Good news. I had wild alone ball dancing through Picassos and Arps and Ernsts with Peggy Guggenheim, she digs me much. I told her all about me prison, etc., etc., she will have date with me tomorrow, so all should be nice. She is very sweet person, sad at heart, and old with memories. But I make her happy, she laughs, and thus I am good in that way. We spoke of sex, we spoke of sex, but I don't know what to do about that. She wanted me to stay over the night, but I couldn't, and I didn't, and I am glad because she walked me late at night to the boat to Ansen's, and sat on barge with me and told me great things about she and Beckett and her life, and it was pleasantly sad and good, thus Venice is becoming romantic for me, in this fashion. I will take her on date tomorrow, but I have only two thousand lire left, what to do, what to do. . . . Her dog died, two days ago, she buried it in her garden. What a weird scene. Late at night she led me into the garden with a jug of water, dark it was, and the

moon was bright, she wore my raincoat and with her thin hand led me to the plot of the dog, there past the Brancusi past the Arp past the Giacometti, we came upon the canine grave, and with great solemnity she took the jug from me and poured the water on the grave that covered the dog. It was all very touching. Later in the evening, after she knew all about me, after all the sex talk, I said, "I must go home, but somehow I am a man and feel very unfulfilled," she embraced me, kissed me, and taking my hand we danced the Picassos and Ernsts. Very strange marvelous lady. Didn't you see that in her? How did you miss it? Perhaps you didn't have time, but really she is great, and sad, and does need friends. Not all those creepy painters all the time. I told her painters were making her into a creep, she laughed, led me to the boat, there we sat and when the boat came fifteen minutes later, I kissed her good-bye, while I watched her walk away I saw that she put her hand to her head as though she were in pain. I suddenly realized the plight of the woman by that gesture. She is a liver of life, and life is fading away. That's all there is to it. It is going. God, how painful to see and know and watch it. But I will say funny things, and she will laugh, and who knows what may happen.

In a letter to the poet Ron Loewinsohn, Corso noted Peggy's "butterfly spectacles and streamlined witchy shoes," called her "a great woman," and added that "Venice has become seemingly romantic as she has become a sort of George Sand for me." A month or so later, Corso wrote Lawrence Ferlinghetti to say that Peggy was "a very fine woman," that she had given him a watch and that they had been talking about going to Greece together.

Soon after he wrote Ginsberg about an intense—and inebriated—conversation with Peggy:

Night before last drunk I offered Peggy my soul in exchange for life, she asked why, and I said I want peace in which to write write write, she said all right, then I said but I must have you for life, and she said, but I am 59 years old, I said if she'd mention age again I'd hate her because I hate told age, she said, all right, is it life you want, then I thought awhile and said, I don't know, all I know is I give you my soul, what I wish in return is obituary, it'll come, someday I'll ask you. . . . It was all mad, the evening closed with a long long embrace and kiss on some Piazza. . . . Thus my date with Peggy.

Before long, their high of initial infatuation began to wear off. An argument erupted after Corso called Peggy "an old Jewish mamma" for nattering on about her desire to separate Pegeen and her boyfriend. Peggy "got mad, phttt. Over. . . . Goodbye Greece, she would have taken me, but I ain't no gold digger and I say what I feel. I am proud of myself. Besides I don't need people any more, especially them who can't take truth."

Corso gave Ginsberg an expanded version of these events, one marked by a disenchanted and even jaded view of Peggy's character. In response to Peggy's fixation on saving Pegeen from her lover, Corso offered to take Pegeen to Afghanistan and abandon her there, "pregnant and all, to the hordes." When Peggy asked what he'd want in return for such a favor, he replied, "Crete"—presumably, a reference to the Greek trip she'd promised him.

> She looked hard at me, then burst out with a "How evil can you be!" and rushed out of the house. I fear, what with all her good intention toward artists, she's not too bright. And after all, she helps painters, not poets, she is a business woman, really, for in painters there is a return, the Picasso on her wall will never die, but the book of poems on her shelf, shall; for there is no return.

Corso's surge of bewildered resentment seems either disingenuous or thick-headed, given that he has proposed (however humorously) taking a woman's beloved daughter to Afghanistan and leaving her there, pregnant, in return for a trip to Crete with Mom. Corso also noted that he planned to write a poem in which Peggy and Pegeen would appear as Demeter and Persephone, the earth goddess and her beautiful young daughter kidnapped by the ruler of the Underworld.

A month later, Corso was readmitted into Peggy's good graces, but their relationship had changed. "Am very good friends with Peggy again, she cut my hair. Will be over for supper tonight."

Ultimately their friendship would come to a bad end. Corso was understandably enraged when Peggy and the Dutch artist Guy Harloff threw out Corso's papers when they were cleaning out Alan Ansen's house in 1962. "Scavengers of the arts they are! They have destroyed important history there. A crime it is, a true crime, and they should pay some kind of dues."

Perhaps that subsequent bitterness informed the account of Corso's relationship with Peggy that appears in Ted Morgan's 1988 biography of William Burroughs, *Literary Outlaw*. Corso told Morgan the story as a series of mistakes. First mistake, refusing to sleep with Peggy. Second, complimenting her garden when she took him out to see the grave of her dog. Third, telling Peggy that the German artist Hundertwasser stole the detachable phallus from the Marini statue; she had accused Corso of having done it. And fourth, letting Peggy know that the woman he really desired was not the mother but the daughter, not Demeter but Persephone, not Peggy but Pegeen.

Pegeen

DESPITE THE pleasure that Peggy took in her Venetian social life, in the beauty of her palazzo, and in the privilege of finally being able to live surrounded by her collection, she was almost constantly worried about Pegeen, who was again showing signs of the instability that had plagued her for much of her adult life. Though she had been treated by a series of psychotherapists, no one seemed capable of diagnosing—much less alleviating—Pegeen's misery, nor of sorting out which of its manifestations was cause, which effect. Prone to depression, she was given prescriptions for sedatives and tranquilizers, to which she became addicted. Like both her parents and her brother, she was a heavy drinker. At several points she stopped eating, but again, no one could tell whether this was a symptom of alcoholism, drug abuse, anorexia, or depression, and as so often happens, the lack of a diagnosis encouraged those around her to hope for the best.

Denied, from an early age, the semblance or the prom-
ise of domestic stability, encouraged to become sexually precocious, involved despite herself in the details of her parents' dramas, abandoned by the stepmother she'd loved, having lost the
nanny she adored when her mother fired Doris, Pegeen had
been obliged to compete for her mother's attention with a succession of unofficial and official stepfathers (most problemati-
cally, Max Ernst) with whom her own relationship was unclear.

Ernst appears to have fostered Pegeen's sexual rivalry with
her mother. This is how Jimmy Ernst describes being with
Peggy, Max, and Pegeen on their cross-country trip:

> The cameos and fragments of the entire period are still a
> jumbled mosaic, the pieces of which refuse to stay in place
> because I was so preoccupied watching a staccato of twists,
> eccentricities and combat in the bewildering relationships
> between Max and Peggy, Peggy and her daughter Pegeen,
> Pegeen and Max, and finally all three of them with me as
> a kind of sounding board, battering ram, and totally inept
> arbitrator. Sixteen-year-old Pegeen, very pretty and very
> confused . . . engaged in tearful hostilities with Peggy, as
> well as with Max, in apparent retaliation for her peripatetic
> life in Europe and the uncertain prospect of a future with a
> mother whose emotional insecurity she sensed only too well.

Later, Jimmy Ernst reports on the atmosphere at the breakfast table in the apartment that Peggy shared with Max and
Pegeen. "It was a tiresome recital of petty quarrels that often
ended in smashed dinner plates, slammed doors, and someone rushing out into the night. Friends, old and new, found
themselves, often unwillingly, part of small or large games of
sex-provocation that often resulted in some strange pairings. It
didn't seem at all logical then that I should be the lightning rod
or mediator of these morning-after tempests that might continue for several days."

As the story of Gregory Corso would seem to suggest, mother and daughter were still competing for men. By this point the long-established patterns of bad behavior involving Peggy and Pegeen—intense affection and worry, reckless criticism, dramatic outbursts, sexual competition, and contempt for the other's lovers and husbands—had become intensely destructive to them both.

Anton Gill's assessment of Peggy's maternal skills seems not merely unfair but absurd. "That Peggy was a bad mother is certain; whether she was always deliberately so is a harder charge to lay." It's not at all clear that Peggy was a "bad mother," though she was a self-involved and frequently neglectful one. But despite what Gill suggests, it is untrue that her treatment of Pegeen was that of a sadist, or that Peggy wasn't sincere when she wrote that there was no one in the world she'd loved so much, that Pegeen was the love of her life.

By the early 1950s, Pegeen's marriage to the older and relatively stable Jean Hélion was ending, partly as a consequence of Pegeen's infidelities. During this period, Michael Wishart lived near Hélion and Pegeen, in Paris: "Pegeen's marriage was breaking up. Divorce, that cruel monster whose trained informers lie in wait for signs of stress in every marriage, was already considering the invitation sent out by their sad, mad quarrels. Pegeen, as the stepdaughter of Max Ernst and the daughter of Peggy, the most generous patroness of the major Surrealist painters, had been brought up in a sophisticated and insecure culture. She was mistaken in thinking that she had outgrown her need for the devotion and paternal security which Hélion provided."

Wishart recalls that he and his wife, Anne, used to see Pegeen and Hélion in the "death throes" of their marriage, fighting "in a large penthouse above the Luxembourg gardens; between and during fights they frequently invited us to visit them." Hélion's Communist sympathies had turned his work away from abstraction and "toward rather obviously 'proletarian' subjects. His canvases were taken over by suitably puppet-like workmen wielding spanners, while the bourgeoisie, wearing iron bowler hats, dozed on park benches."

> Meanwhile Pegeen continued to paint, and occasionally to exhibit (notably in Milan with an excellent foreword in the catalogue by the late Sir Herbert Read) her mysterious pictures. These consisted chiefly in her evocation of the nurseries and Venetian scenes which were her daily background; but presented as though everything, including Pegeen, her children, her pets, gondolas and gondoliers, had been made from barley sugar. Her paintings recreated an entire world as though composed of the spiral reflections of those multi-colored posts to which gondolas are tethered, wobbling in wait for their aristocratic owners.

Not long after the birth of her third son, Nicolas, in 1952, Pegeen began a love affair with an Italian artist, Tancredi, one of her mother's protégés. He'd occupied the studio beside Pegeen's in the basement of Peggy's palazzo, so it could be claimed that Peggy played a part in bringing them together. The romance was more serious than any of the affairs Pegeen had had while she was with Hélion, and it helped end the marriage. After Pegeen and Tancredi separated, Tancredi left Venice for Rome, married, had children, and drowned himself in the Tiber.

Around this time, Peggy decided to take Pegeen to London, apparently hoping that Pegeen might meet a wealthy and stable British aristocrat to marry. If that was Peggy's intention, it soon backfired. Within days of their arrival, Pegeen met, and fell madly in love with, the British painter Ralph Rumney, who was almost ten years younger than Pegeen, whose drinking equaled or outmatched hers, and who was by no means a model of emotional stability. The son of a vicar, Rumney had been ousted from the Young Communists League and was later expelled from the Situationist International, a radical art-political group that combined elements of Marxism with Surrealist theory.

To an outside observer, Rumney seems to have possessed something of the arty, impractical charisma with which Peggy had so often fallen in love. But Peggy had learned her lesson about such men, even if her daughter hadn't. Peggy disliked and distrusted Rumney and soon came to see him as a gold-digger and (despite the fact that Pegeen had been unhappy for so long) as the cause of all Pegeen's unhappiness. In 1958, Pegeen gave birth to Rumney's child, a boy named Sandro; the arrival of her grandson failed to soften Peggy's view of Rumney, to whom she offered a lot of money—which he refused—to leave Pegeen.

But Peggy was not so distracted by Pegeen's problems that she didn't continue collecting art. In 1954, she bought René Magritte's *Empire of Light*, and three years afterward she added paintings by Paul Jenkins, Ben Nicholson, and Francis Bacon to her collection. Later she would buy works by Dubuffet, de Kooning, and a number of Italian artists. Meanwhile, she continued to make new friends: John Cage brought the dancer Merce Cunningham to stay with Peggy, and they introduced her to the Japanese-American performance artist Yoko Ono; Peggy, Ono, and Cage traveled together through Japan. In New York, in 1959, Peggy visited Frank Lloyd Wright's as yet uncompleted building, commissioned to showcase the art collected by her Uncle Solomon, who had died a decade before. Peggy was unimpressed by the structure, which she called "Uncle Solomon's garage."

Two years later, Peggy again returned to New York, this time to sue Lee Krasner for having defrauded her by concealing the existence of a small trove of art that Pollock had created while under contract to Peggy—and that belonged to her. Ultimately, the suit was settled, and Peggy was awarded $122,000.

Peggy remained obsessed with Ralph Rumney, whom she refused to see or speak to, and whom she accused of having made Pegeen pregnant so that she would stay with him and support him. The couple lived in romantic and uncomfortable bohemian poverty, splitting their time between Venice and Paris. After their marriage in 1958, they moved to Paris, where they bought a small apartment with the proceeds from the sale of a Max Ernst painting that had belonged to Pegeen.

According to Michael Wishart, "I had been devoted to Pegeen since our childhood, and it was terrible to see her gradually overwhelmed by a confusion and despair which were to drive her, after several unsuccessful attempts, to take her life. After her divorce Pegeen married the handsome and brilliant if erratic English artist Ralph Rumney, who added another son to her large brood, but who was unable to help her in the wildness of disappointment and despair to which life had driven this exquisite and delicate temperament. I can never recall Pegeen's long golden hair without thinking of Ophelia."

Meanwhile, Peggy was growing increasingly concerned about what would happen to her collection after her death. In *Peggy Guggenheim and Her Friends* her sister Hazel rather mischievously recalls Peggy's promising that Pegeen would inherit the collection and be its curator after Peggy's death. But Pegeen, writes Hazel, was upset because Peggy told her that she wouldn't be allowed to touch or change anything, not one painting.

After considerable dithering about the foundation she wished to establish and about who would sit on the board, Peggy instructed Bernard Reis to draw up a will leaving everything she owned—except the palazzo and the collection—to her children, who would be obliged to renounce all claims to their mother's art. In 1964, she shipped her collection to London, where it was the subject of a popular show at the Tate Gallery. Pegeen and Sindbad came to London to share in their mother's glory and to enjoy a rare moment of family harmony.

As Pegeen's depression and substance abuse worsened, Rumney began to behave in ways frighteningly reminiscent of the young Laurence Vail. Ralph could be charming and articulate, but he became argumentative and violent when he drank. Pegeen's relationship with her mother veered between closeness and estrangement, as Pegeen alternately confided in Peggy and refused to speak to her. Pegeen spent time in clinics; at one point Laurence and Ralph attempted to curb her addictions by locking her in a room—a treatment that predictably failed.

In February 1967, Ralph was arrested in Venice and jailed overnight for reasons not entirely clear. Later, he claimed that Peggy had arranged his detention and his subsequent expulsion from Italy. The incident terrified Pegeen, who (wrongly) interpreted it to mean that she too would never be allowed to return to Venice.

On the night Rumney returned to Paris, he and Pegeen argued until Pegeen was too exhausted to continue fighting—and she went off to sleep in the maid's room. The next morning, Ralph left to take the boys to school. He returned home and fell asleep; when he woke again, Pegeen failed to respond to his knock on the door. He managed to retrieve the key, unlocked the door—and found Pegeen dead.

Traveling in Mexico, Peggy was worried enough about Pegeen to light a candle for her when her friend Robert Brady took her to visit the church of Santa Maria Tonantzintla. Brady recalls, "I opened a telegram and I turned green. She knew it was about Pegeen. The telegram read: 'Pegeen deceased. Come to Paris immediately.' She told me later that she lit the candle the same moment as Pegeen's death. We spoke all night and she never broke down. She was the bravest woman in the world."

Once more it seems wise to let Peggy have the last word, this time about her daughter.

> I went to visit Robert Brady in Mexico, and that is where I was when I got the tragic news of Pegeen's death. My darling Pegeen, who was not only a daughter, but also a mother, a friend and a sister to me. We seemed also to have had a perpetual love affair. Her untimely and mysterious death left me quite desolate. There was no one in the world I loved so much. I felt all the light had gone out of my life. Pegeen was a most talented primitive painter. For years I had fostered her talent and sold her paintings. She was just beginning to have a real success, having shows that winter in Canada, Stockholm and Philadelphia.

Peggy intended this as an expression of the purest love and devotion, but everything about it seems slightly off, misguided. It is wise to see a daughter as a mother, a sister and a friend? Wouldn't it have been better to see her simply as a daughter? Peggy's friend Nellie van Doesburg describes the mother and daughter as "sisterly." All of this suggests an ongoing problem in Peggy's relationship with Pegeen: the mother's penchant for involving the daughter in her romantic dramas, the way one might sensibly involve a sister or a friend, as well as her habit of falling back on Pegeen, obliging her to assume the comforting maternal role in the aftermath of Peggy's romantic disasters, most notably her failed marriage to Max Ernst. And isn't it odd for a mother to describe her relationship with her daughter as a "perpetual love affair," especially when that mother has had a history of stormy and disappointing romances?

Peggy tells us more about her own desolation than about the daughter she lost. And ending the passage by praising Pegeen's talent as a "primitive painter" who has shown in Canada, Stockholm, and Philadelphia brings to mind the charge, so often leveled at Peggy, that the neglected Pegeen had become an artist in an attempt to get the attention of a mother who referred to her paintings as her children and to the refugee artists she helped as her babies.

So Peggy memorialized her daughter by praising her art career. She mentions none of her strong points, her character traits or virtues, or even the fact that she herself was a mother. As skilled a writer as Peggy was, her elegy for Pegeen omits all the elements one might wish for in a eulogy: a sense of what the person was like, of what it was like to know her. It is more like a résumé.

Slightly later in her memoir, disputing the inaccuracies in John Davis's *The Guggenheims: An American Epic,* a book she loathed, Peggy wrote, "There is no proof that Pegeen committed suicide. The doctor who performed the autopsy said that she died from her lungs. I think she must have suffocated from her vomit." Of course, it is rare to choke on one's own vomit unless one is heavily under the influence of alcohol or drugs or both. Michael Wishart wrote, "She was using too many pills and visited me without warning at all hours of the night, usually in tears."

Though it is commonly assumed that Pegeen's death was the result of an overdose of some sort, it is impossible to determine whether it was accidental, impulsive, or calculated; those who argue for the latter view cite the numerous suicide attempts that Pegeen had made in the past. One friend reported attending a garden party at which Pegeen appeared, from beyond the edge of the lawn, completely covered in blood. Another story describes Pegeen announcing to a dinner party that she was going off to the bathroom to kill herself, a statement that most took as a joke until she swallowed an entire vial of pills. One hears people say with confidence that Pegeen was murdered, but in the absence of a thorough investigation, this explanation for her death seems unlikely.

By the time she wrote the final version of *Out of This Century*, Peggy had grown more careful. All she says about Ralph Rumney occurs in the course of refuting the charge, leveled in John Davis's book, that she was stingy with her children. "I gave a large regular allowance to Pegeen and Sindbad and sold many paintings for Pegeen in my gallery. If she was short of money it was because her husband Ralph Rumney provided nothing and spent fortunes." Peggy's grievances against Rumney seem to be economic and therefore mild compared to her real feeling, which was that Rumney was to blame for her daughter's death. At first she tried to have Ralph charged with Pegeen's murder; when that failed she arranged for him to be charged with neglecting to come to the aid of a person in mortal danger: a crime in France. Ralph escaped Paris—and the police—by seeking refuge in a clinic run by Feliz Guattari, a politically radical psychotherapist and student of Lacan's. By the time Ralph returned to England, the Guggenheims and Vails had taken his son Sandro, whom he would not see for another ten years.

In the Peggy Guggenheim Collection there is a room dedicated to the memory—and the work—of Pegeen. The brightly colored paintings possess a wistful innocence, a dreamy make-believe; they seem to be the product of a touching effort to recapture the simplicity and spontaneity of childhood. Certain passages of the paintings look more Haitian than Venetian. Knowing about Pegeen's sad life, we may find it hard to avoid reading melancholy into these images, a longing to escape and live among the happy families, the innocent lovers, the cartoonish sweetness she created.

The most striking thing about the room is the photograph of Pegeen. However physically and psychologically different we imagine the mother and daughter to have been—Peggy with her dyed black bob and slash of red lipstick, Pegeen with her long blond hair; the forceful, willful, outspoken mother and the shy, damaged Ophelia-like daughter—the fact is that Pegeen strongly resembles her mother. It's not so much a physical likeness (though there is that, too) as a similarity of gesture. Pegeen's hand is raised to her throat, her chin tucked slightly in, like a bird's into its breast, as if—like her mother—she were just on the point of speaking and is hesitating for an instant, momentarily worried—as her mother so often was, especially as a young woman—about how her remarks will be received.

A Death in Venice

PEGGY OUTLIVED her daughter by twelve years. Much of that time was spent making a final determination about her legacy. In 1969, New York's Guggenheim Museum showed a large part of Peggy's collection. Though she felt that the building dwarfed and overshadowed the paintings—a complaint that would be made about other shows at the museum—she was pleased by the enthusiasm of the press, and by the fact that her art was being exhibited at her uncle's museum. Later that month, she decided to transfer the collection to the Guggenheim Foundation, which would safeguard it in Venice. She made the transfer in 1976.

During Peggy's final years, her health declined. She suffered from arteriosclerosis and was often in pain. She had high blood pressure and survived a heart attack and several serious falls. She still took pleasure in entertaining and seeing friends, and especially in traveling, by gondola, all over Venice—an experience she wrote about beautifully in the third, most complete and exuberant version of her memoir, which she worked on through the 1970s and which was published just before her death, from a stroke, in December 1979.

> It is always assumed that Venice is the ideal place for a honeymoon. This is a grave error. To live in Venice or even to visit it means that you fall in love with the city itself. There is nothing left over in your heart for anyone else. After your first visit you are destined to return at every possible chance or with every possible excuse.

The last chapter of Peggy's memoir contains some of the best writing that has ever been done about Venice, a city about which so much has been written. "There is no normal life in Venice. Here everything and everyone floats. . . . One floats in and out of restaurants, shops, cinemas, theaters, museums, churches and hotels. . . . It is this floatingness which is the essential quality of Venice."

With her gift for language, the talent for which she is so rarely credited, Peggy Guggenheim described the rhythm of rising and falling tides, the clamor of the church bells, the way in which one is always conscious of history, always catching glimpses "of the past alive with romance, elopements, abductions, revenged passions, intrigues, adulteries, denoucements, unaccountable deaths, gambling, lute playing and singing." And no one has more accurately described the Venetian light that Canaletto captured in his paintings. "As the hours progress the light becomes more and more violet until it envelops the city with a diamond-like haze. . . . If anything can rival Venice in its beauty, it must be its reflection at sunset in the Grand Canal."

Today, visitors to the Peggy Guggenheim Collection can admire the combination of modernity and tradition that make the museum unlike any other. The height and the generous dimensions of the rooms and the intact fireplaces suggest the palazzo's origins in the eighteenth century, but the gilt and scrollwork that characterize so many Venetian interiors are absent, and the plain white walls are ideally suited to the art they display.

One feels the evidence of Peggy's spirit and presence everywhere. Her gravestone is in the garden, alongside another plaque that reads, "Here lie my beloved babies," and lists her cherished dogs, many of whom she named after friends and relatives. The inscription on a stone bench made by Jenny Holzer, donated to the Solomon R. Guggenheim Foundation after Peggy's death, sounds like something that Peggy herself would have said: "Savor kindness because cruelty is always possible later."

But of course the most extraordinary feature of the palazzo, and the reason to visit, is Peggy's magnificent collection. One can't help being struck by Peggy Guggenheim's extraordinary eye, by the amazing array of art that she was able to accumulate, and by the wisdom and perspicacity she showed in finding (and listening to) a succession of knowledgeable and helpful advisers.

In the entrance hall are canvases by Picasso and a Calder mobile. Elsewhere are paintings by Ernst, Miró, Kandinsky, Malevich, Klee, Mondrian, Léger, Braque, Mark Rothko, Clyfford Still, Francis Bacon, and, of course, Jackson Pollock, represented here by several works, including the 1947 *Alchemy*, one of his earliest poured paintings. There are also mementos celebrating Peggy's personal and professional connections with artists: the lovely silver headboard she had made for her by Alexander Calder, the splashy and dramatic earrings that Calder and Yves Tanguy fashioned especially for her, and which she wore to the opening of her Art of This Century gallery.

To visit the Peggy Guggenheim Collection is to be moved, impressed—amazed—by how much she accomplished. The structure itself is beautiful, reflecting the changes Peggy made;

one of the most significant was to tear away the vines that covered the somewhat severe white stone façade. That confident, slightly reckless, ingeniously subtle melding of centuries continues throughout the museum, in the nobly Venetian proportions of the room, stripped of the flocked and gilded Venetian esthetic, and painted white to better display its Picassos and Pollocks, its Brancusis and Calders and Braques.

The Palazzo Venier dei Leoni represents the culmination of Peggy Guggenheim's particular talents, among them her ability to locate extraordinary homes and adapt them to suit her needs. The house she shared with Laurence Vail in the south of France; Hayford Hall, where she lived with John Ferrar Holmes; the baronial East Side apartment in Manhattan in which her marriage to Max Ernst limped along and collapsed—all were surpassed by the palace for which she had waited for years, biding her time until she found the right one. Her palazzo is in the Dorsoduro, a lovely neighborhood near the Accademia Galleries, and, except at the height of the tourist season, relatively quiet.

In its current incarnation, the Peggy Guggenheim Collection invites you into a sequence of beautiful but modest rooms in which there is little danger (as Peggy feared there would be, in her 57th Street gallery) of the setting competing with the art. One is frequently struck by the fact that one person, aided by her advisers, managed to put all this together. Not only is there an astonishing quantity of first-rate art, by so many great artists, but each work seems exemplary: capable of repaying however much time and attention the viewer chooses to give it.

Indeed, the challenge is to stay focused, because even as one is staring at a marvelous Picasso, one might become aware of a Miró, and drift from that to a Paul Klee, or a Francis Bacon. It's possible to spend hours contemplating each of the Jackson Pollocks. But there is Brancusi's *Bird in Space*, and on the mantel of a fireplace is a Joseph Cornell box containing a magical diorama: a fairy-tale chateau and bare wintry trees. The mostly young, international staff seems appreciative of the opportunity to work at what they know is one of the world's most significant collections of modern art.

A bright-eyed, soft-spoken man, Philip Rylands meets me in the modern café facing the museum's garden. He readily confirms the view of Peggy I'd formed from my reading and research—a more sympathetic picture than one finds in some of her biographies, such as Anton Gill's harshly judgmental *Art Lover*, and her unflattering appearances in fiction, among them in Mary McCarthy's short story "The Cicerone."

"She was very modest," Rylands says, "and yet she made an astonishing mark on the twentieth century by amassing one of the most remarkable and outstanding collections of modern art. She was fascinated by people and how they interacted. That was part of the reason why she had the most international salon in Venice. Part of her zest for human interaction was about her desire to really get to know other people. She was never banal, never said anything that seemed like a cliché. When she spoke it was a direct expression of her thoughts, and she thought a great deal. She did have the rich person's fear of being taken advantage of, but she was generous—generous to her children and grandchildren and to artists and writers she supported and admired."

When I ask him what he most wants to say about Peggy Guggenheim, what he feels should be emphasized, he says, "Well, I suppose the most important thing one can say is to quote Lee Krasner:

" 'She did it.' "

It's Carnevale in Venice, and I've stopped to rest at a café on the edge of the Campo Sant'Aponal, partly to celebrate finding my way after having been lost for quite a while and partly because one of the tables is full of Venetian kids dressed as 1920s Chicago gangsters. It's fun to watch them smoke Gauloises and talk out of the sides of their mouths in what they imagine as the style of Al Capone.

When the proprietor (whose festival attire includes a large polka-dotted bow tie) brings my coffee and *fritelle*, a fried pastry filled with lemon cream, popular at the holiday season, he asks where I'm from. Ah, New York. A beautiful city. Thank you, I say, then make the obvious reply: Venice is also a beautiful city. Ah, but New York, New York has been the home of Jasper Johns, Franz Kline. Robert Rauschenberg. Have I heard of Robert Rauschenberg? I tell him yes, I know a little about art, in fact I've come to Venice to write about Peggy Guggenheim . . .

His face lights up. "Ah," he says. *"La Peggy!"*

He tells me how, as a young man—*a young artist*—he used to stand and wave to *la Peggy* as she glided by, making her nightly pleasure cruise, by private gondola, through the narrow canals, with her little dog in her lap. Her Peekeen-ay-zee! Did I know that she brought modern art to Venice, that she changed the city forever, that it is only because of *la Peggy* that Italians first learned about Abstract Expressionism? Have I been to her museum? Have I seen the Jackson Pollocks?

Inside the café, he shows me, on the wall, a photo of Peggy Guggenheim, elderly and rather beautiful—in some ways more beautiful than she was as a younger woman. Her white hair is carefully done, she wears, regally, a metallic gold dress, her fluffy white dog nestles her lap.

In the photo, as in a film of her made late in life, *L'Ultima Dogaressa*, Peggy manages to project the regal entitlement of an elderly queen combined with the self-consciousness of a nervous girl. I don't have the heart to tell *la Peggy*'s admirer that the dog is not a Peekeen-ay-zee, but a Lhasa Apso.

Almost forty years after her death, Peggy Guggenheim is a hero to many Venetians, among them the art-loving café owner.

Peggy Guggenheim acquired extraordinary works of art, she assembled a major collection, she saved it and kept it together through some very difficult situations, she moved more than a hundred paintings and sculptures from one continent to another until she found a city that people would always visit, where the beauty of the city would make people want to look at art, at work that is more modern but no less inspired than the Titians and Tintorettos, at a collection that represents a long and glorious chapter in the history that goes back to the Chauvet cave paintings and forward into the future.

A NOTE ON SOURCES

I HAVE quoted liberally from Peggy Guggenheim's memoir, *Out of This Century*, which was first published in 1946 and reissued, with significant additions and with the real names of people (changed in the first edition) restored, in 1979, the year of its author's death. Peggy's charming, humorous, and peculiar literary voice is as revealing of her character as any of the events she describes, and I highly recommend her book. But since it seems clear that Peggy sometimes preferred the good story to the strictly accurate one, I have consulted the numerous books of nonfiction and fiction that have been written about (or based on) her eventful career.

The earliest of the biographies, Jacqueline Bograd Weld's *Peggy: The Wayward Guggenheim*, was authorized by Peggy Guggenheim and is written in an appealingly conversational, gossipy tone. A more recent and comprehensive biography is Mary V. Dearborn's well-researched and elegantly written *Mistress of Modernism*, published in 2004 and, sadly, now out of print. The only long biography now available in print is Anton Gill's *Art Lover*, which provides interesting anecdotes and information but which often betrays a disapproving and contemptuous opinion of its subject.

An invaluable resource has been the handsome, lavishly illustrated, and extremely informative *Peggy Guggenheim and Frederick Kiesler: The Story of Art of This Century*, edited by Susan Davidson and Philip Rylands. The book includes a highly compressed yet thorough and lucid biographical essay by Rylands. Other essays focus on the career of Frederick Kiesler, who designed Peggy's Art of This Century gallery, and on his work with Peggy. Remarkably, the book contains an account of every show that appeared in the Daylight Gallery during the life of Art of This Century, from a consideration of the works on display to the critical reception to the guests who attended the opening reception. The generous selection of photographs and architectural drawings tells us as much as can be known about the experience of visiting the gallery.

The best way to appreciate the extent and the brilliance of Peggy Gugghenheim's collection is, of course, to see it in Venice. Short of that, one can read with pleasure Angelica Zander Rudenstine's lavishly illustrated, substantial, and authoritative catalogue raisonné of the collection.

One measure of the breadth and brilliance of Peggy's acquaintanceship was the number of biographies in which she appears. I accumulated an entire shelf of books about people who knew Peggy. Among the most notable of these are *Duchamp*, by Calvin Tompkins; *Samuel Beckett*, by Deirdre Bair; *Becoming Modern: The Life of Mina Loy*, by Carolyn Burke; *Kay Boyle: Author of Herself*, by Joan Mellen; Millicent Dillon's *A Little Original Sin: The Life and Work of Jane Bowles*; and two biographies of Djuna Barnes, by Andrew Field and Philip Herring. Especially interesting are the books about, and the books that came out of, the years when Peggy shared a house in the British countryside with a revolving cast of women writers. Edited by Elizabeth Podnieks, *Rough Draft*, Emily Coleman's passionate, lively journals, was a revelation.

Peggy also appears, more or less disguised, in fiction and memoir. Mary McCarthy's "The Cicerone" features Peggy thinly masked as Polly Grabbe and provides a uniquely fleshed out and (for my purposes) useful view of how Peggy appeared to friends who actually didn't much like her. Her portrait, as Molly, in William Gerhardie's *Of Mortal Love* is only marginally more flattering but equally revealing.

Several of the most entertaining and helpful books in which Peggy appears are memoirs. Jimmy Ernst's *A Not-So-Still Life* is almost uniquely understanding and compassionate in its view of Peggy and gives a vivid sense of the early days of Art of This Century and of her difficult marriage to Jimmy's father, Max. Reissued by New York Review Books, John Glassco's novel-memoir *Memoirs of Montparnasse* provides a lively picture of Paris during the era, and, more briefly, of Peggy and Laurence Vail. Michael Wishart's *High Diver* is a book that should be in print; it's a witty, sympathetic, and gossipy autobiography by a man who knew as many (and some of the same) interesting characters as did Peggy.

Finally, *An Accidental Autobiography: The Selected Letters of Gregory Corso*, edited by Bill Morgan, offers an intimate and quite beautiful account of what it was like to be the object of Peggy's romantic interest, late in her life.

BIBLIOGRAPHY

Bair, Deirdre. *Samuel Beckett: A Biography.* 1978; rpt. New York: Simon and Schuster, 1990.

Barnes, Djuna. *Nightwood.* 1937; rpt. New York: New Directions, 2006.

Beckett, Samuel. *The Letters of Samuel Beckett: Volume 1, 1929–40.* New York: Cambridge University Press, 2009.

Benstock, Shari. *Women of the Left Bank: Paris, 1900–1940.* Austin: University of Texas Press, 1987.

Bernier, Rosamund. *Some of My Lives: A Scrapbook Memoir.* New York: Farrar, Straus and Giroux, 2011.

Birmingham, Stephen. *Our Crowd: The Great Jewish Families of New York.* 1967; rpt. Syracuse, N.Y.: Syracuse University Press, 1996.

Bowles, Jane. *Two Serious Ladies.* 1943; rpt. New York: Ecco, 2014.

Burke, Carolyn. *Becoming Modern: The Life of Mina Loy.* New York: Farrar, Straus and Giroux, 1996.

Coleman, Emily. *Rough Draft: The Modernist Diaries of Emily Holmes Coleman, 1929–1937.* Ed. Elizabeth Podnieks and Sandra Chair. Newark: University of Delaware Press, 2012.

————. *The Shutter of Snow.* 1930; rpt. Champaign, Ill.: Dalkey Archive, 2007.

Corso, Gregory. *An Accidental Autobiography: The Selected Letters of Gregory Corso.* Ed. Bill Morgan. New York: New Directions, 2003.

Cronin, Anthony. *Samuel Beckett: The Last Modernist.* 1997; rpt. New York: Da Capo, 1999.

Davidson, Susan, and Philip Rylands, eds. *Peggy Guggenheim and Frederick Kiesler: The Story of Art of This Century.* Venice: Peggy Guggenheim Collection, 2004.

Davis, John H. *The Guggenheims, 1848–1988: An American Epic.* New York: William Morrow, 1988.

Dearborn, Mary V. *Mistress of Modernism: The Life of Peggy Guggenheim.* Boston: Houghton Mifflin, 2004.

Dillon, Millicent. *A Little Original Sin: The Life and Work of Jane Bowles.* New York: Holt, Rinehart and Winston, 1981.

Dortch, Virginia M., ed. *Peggy Guggenheim and Her Friends.* Milan: Berenice, 1994.

Ernst, Jimmy. *A Not-So-Still Life: A Child of Europe's Pre–World War II Art World and His Remarkable Homecoming to America.* New York: St. Martin's, 1984.

Field, Andrew. *Djuna: The Life and Times of Djuna Barnes.* New York: G. P. Putnam's Sons, 1983.

Gerhardie, William. *Of Mortal Love.* 1925; rpt. New York: St. Martin's, 1947.

Gill, Anton. *Art Lover: A Biography of Peggy Guggenheim.* New York: HarperCollins, 2002.

Glassco, John. *Memoirs of Montparnasse.* New York: Oxford University Press, 1970; rpt. New York: New York Review Books, 2007.

Goldman, Emma. *Living My Life.* 1931–34; rpt. New York: Penguin Books, 2006.

Goldstein, Malcolm. *Landscape with Figures: A History of Art Dealing in the United States.* New York: Oxford University Press, 2000.

Guggenheim, Peggy. *Out of This Century.* New York: Dial, 1946; rev. and expanded ed. New York: Universe, 1979.

———. *Confessions of an Art Addict*. 1960; New York: Ecco, 1997.

Herring, Philip. *Djuna: The Life and Work of Djuna Barnes*. New York: Viking, 1995.

Jenison, Madge. *Sunwise Turn: A Human Comedy of Bookselling*. New York: Dutton, 1924.

Josephson, Matthew. *Life Among the Surrealists*. New York: Holt, Rinehart and Winston, 1962.

Kiernan, Frances. *Seeing Mary Plain: The Life of Mary McCarthy*. New York: Norton, 2002.

Levin, Gail. *Lee Krasner: A Biography*. New York: William Morrow, 2011.

Mann, Carol. *Paris Between the Wars*. New York: Vendome, 1996.

McCarthy, Mary. *Cast a Cold Eye*. 1950; rpt. New York: Harcourt Brace, 1992.

Mellen, Joan. *Kay Boyle: Author of Herself*. New York: Farrar, Straus and Giroux, 1994.

Morgan, Ted. *Literary Outlaw: The Life and Times of William S. Burroughs*. New York: Holt, 1988.

Muir, Edwin. *An Autobiography*. St. Paul, Minn.: Graywolf, 1990.

Podnieks, Elizabeth, and Sandra Chair, eds. *Hayford Hall: Hangovers, Erotics, and Modernist Aesthetics*. Carbondale: Southern Illinois University Press, 2005.

Polizzotti, Mark. *Revolution of the Mind: The Life of André Breton*. New York: Farrar, Straus and Giroux, 1995.

Riding, Alan. *And the Show Went On: Cultural Life in Nazi-Occupied Paris*. New York: Knopf, 2010.

Rudenstine, Angelica. *Peggy Guggenheim Collection, Venice, the Solomon R. Guggenheim Foundation*. New York: Harry Abrams, 1985.

Russell, John. *Max Ernst: Life and Work*. New York: Abrams, 1967.

Sawyer-Laucanno, Christopher. *An Invisible Spectator: A Biography of Paul Bowles*. New York: Weidenfeld and Nicolson, 1989.

Solomon, Deborah. *Jackson Pollock: A Biography*. New York: Simon and Schuster, 1987.

Tanning, Dorothea. *Birthday*. San Francisco: Lapis, 1986.

Tomkins, Calvin. *Duchamp: A Biography*. New York: Henry Holt, 1996.

Vail, Laurence. *Murder! Murder!* London: Peter Davies, 1931.

Weld, Jacqueline Bograd. *Peggy: The Wayward Guggenheim.* New York: Dutton, 1986.

Wishart, Michael. *High Diver: An Autobiography.* London: Quartet, 1978.

CREDITS

Peggy Guggenheim, numerous excerpts throughout, from *Confessions of an Art Addict*, copyright © 1960 by Peggy Guggenheim. Foreword copyright © 1979 by Gore Vidal. Reprinted by permission of HarperCollins Publishers.

Emily Coleman, excerpts from *Rough Draft: The Modernist Diaries of Emily Holmes Coleman, 1929–1937*, edited by Elizabeth Podnieks and Sandra Chair (Newark: University of Delaware Press, 2012). Reprinted with the permission of the Estate of Emily Holmes Coleman.

Excerpts from the letters of Gregory Corso (pp. 170–72), from *An Accidental Autobiography*, Copyright © 2003 by New Directions Publishing Corp. Reprinted by permission of New Directions Publishing Corp.

Virginia M. Dortch, excerpts from *Peggy Guggenheim and Her Friends* (Milan: Berenice, 1994). Copyright © 1994 by Virginia M. Dortch. Reprinted with the permission of the Estate of Virginia M. Dortch.

Figure 1: Photograph by Man Ray. Copyright © Man Ray Trust /
Artists Rights Society (ARS), NY / ADAGP, Paris / Telimage,
Paris 2015.

Figure 2: Photograph courtesy of Clover Vail.

Figure 3: Photograph courtesy of University of Maryland Librar-
ies, Special Collections and University Archives.

Figure 4: Photograph by Rogi André. Bibliothèque National de
France (BnF). Copyright © BnF, Dist. RMN-Grand Palace /
Art Resource, NY.

Figure 5: Unknown photographer. Gift of Jacqueline, Paul, and
Peter Matisse in memory of their mother, Alexina Duchamp.
Photograph courtesy of Philadelphia Museum of Art, Archives.

Figure 6: Photograph courtesy of Solomon R. Guggenheim Museum Photo Archives, New York.

Figure 7: Photograph by George Karger, courtesy of Solomon R.
Guggenheim Museum Archives, New York.

Figure 8: Photograph by Benjamin Hélion. Reprinted through Cre-
ative Commons license, http://creativecommons.org/licenses/
by-sa/3.0), photo via Wikimedia Commons.

Figure 9: Photograph courtesy of Archivio Cameraphoto Epoche.
Gift, Cassa di Risparmio di Venezia, 2005. Solomon R. Guggenheim Foundation.

Figure 10: Photograph courtesy of Solomon R. Guggenheim Museum Photo Archives, New York.

Figure 11: Copyright © Solomon R. Guggenheim Foundation,
NY.

INDEX